that
kind of girl

CW00952668

EROS COMIX™, P.O. Box 25070, Seattle, WA 98125.
Edited by Ezra Mark. Art direction by Brad Angell. Published by Gary Groth and Kim Thompson. *That Kind of Girl* is copyright © 1999 Molly Kiely. All rights reserved. Permission to quote or reproduce material for reviews or notices must be obtained from Eros Comix™, in writing, at P.O. Box 25070, Seattle WA 98125. Check out the Eros website: http://www.eroscomix.com. This graphic novel is under no circumstances to be sold to persons under 18 years of age. First Eros Comix™ edition: July, 1999. ISBN: 1-56097-375-7. Printed in Hong Kong.

that kind of girl

by Molly Kiely

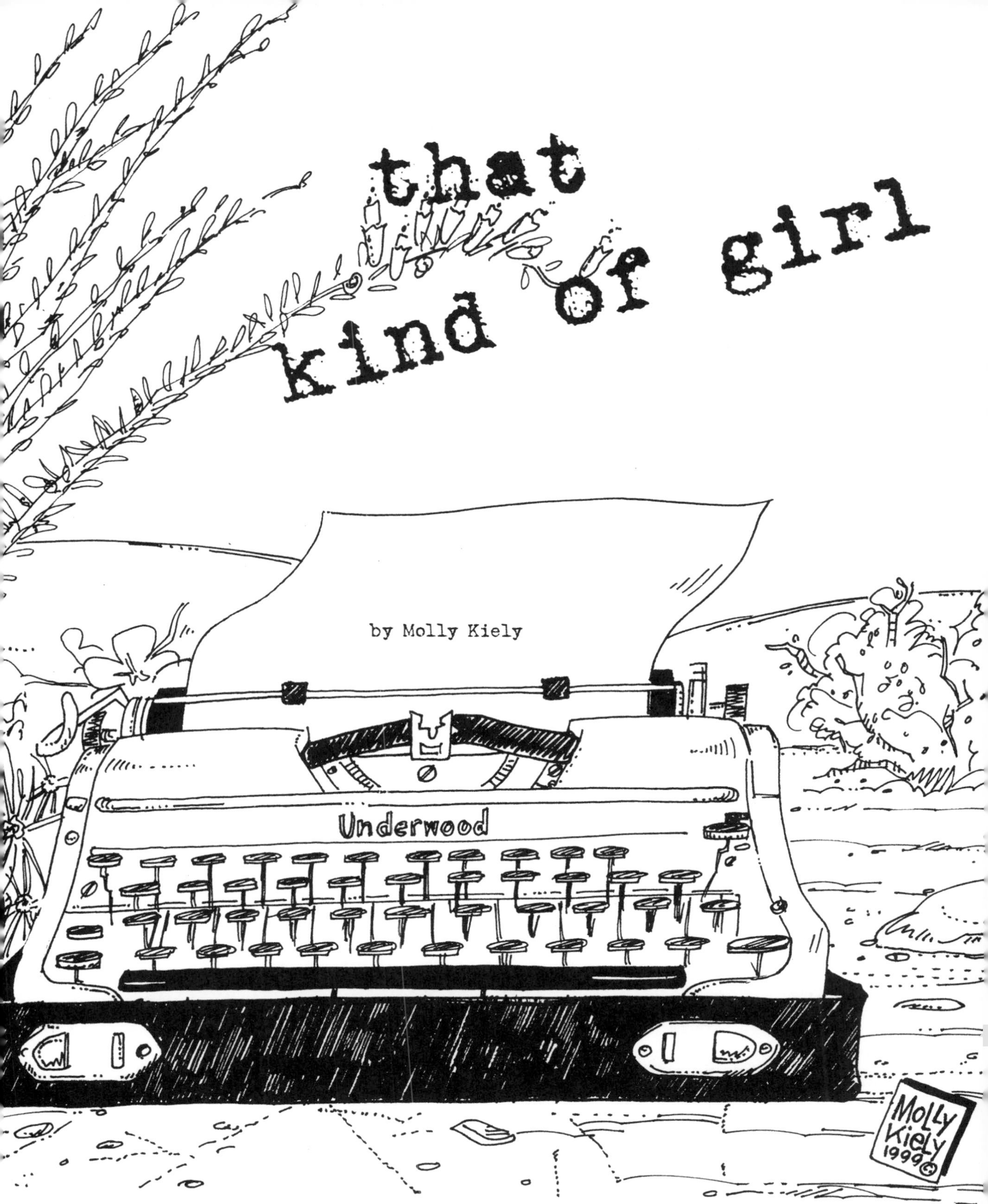
Underwood
MOLLY KIELY 1999 ©

EROS™ COMIX

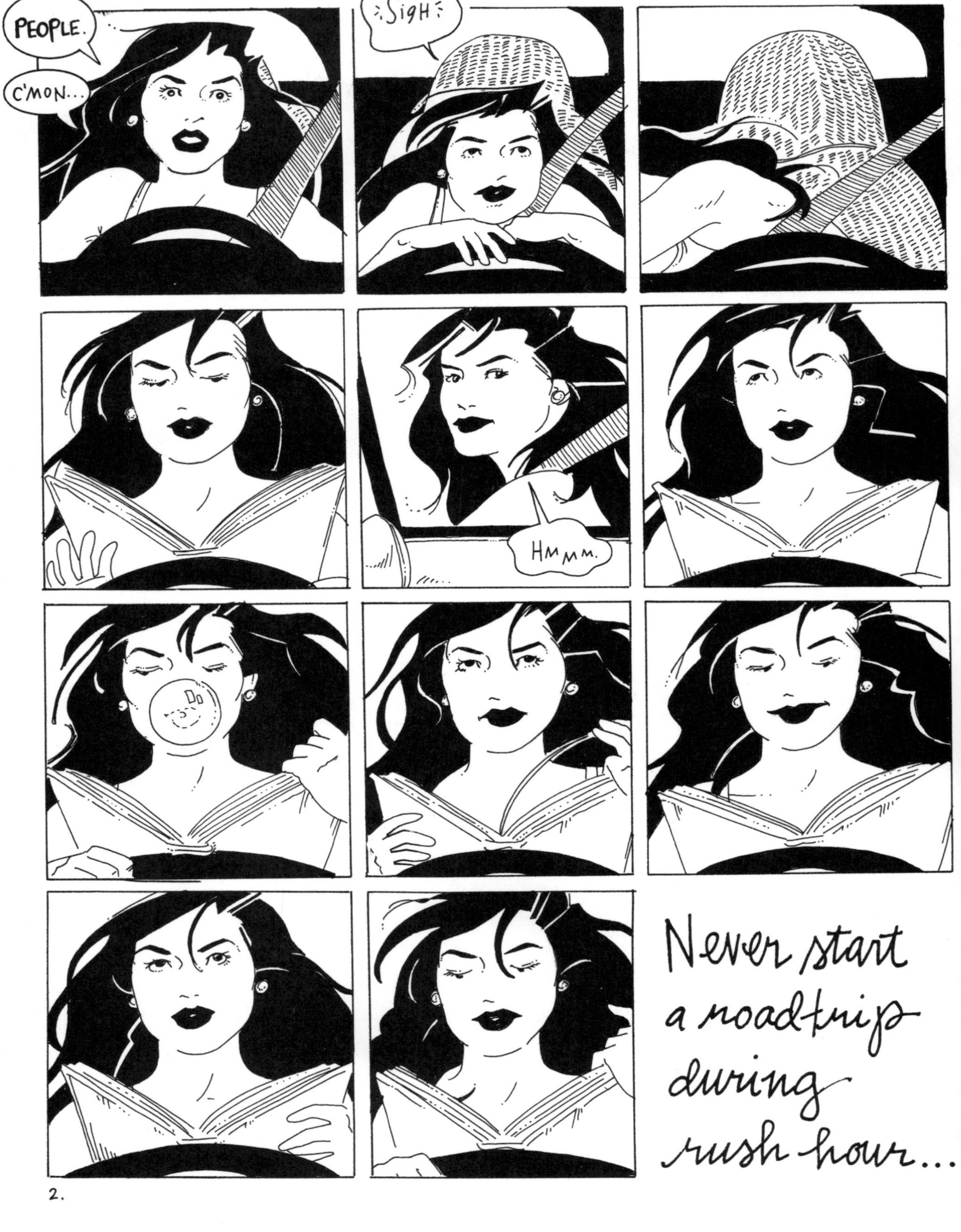
PEOPLE.
C'MON...
SIGH
HMMM.
Never start a roadtrip during rush hour...

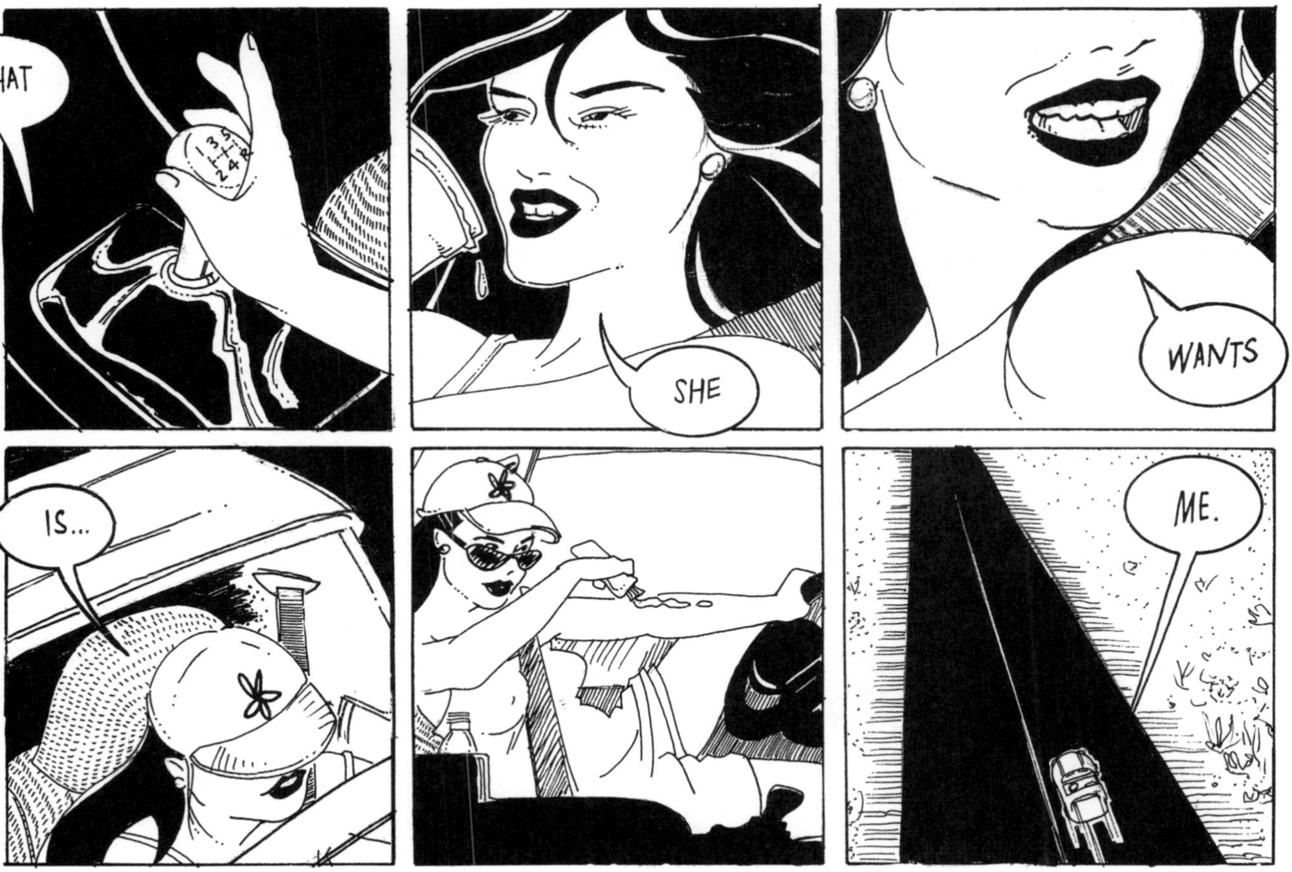
WHAT
SHE
WANTS
IS...
ME.

Finally moving...

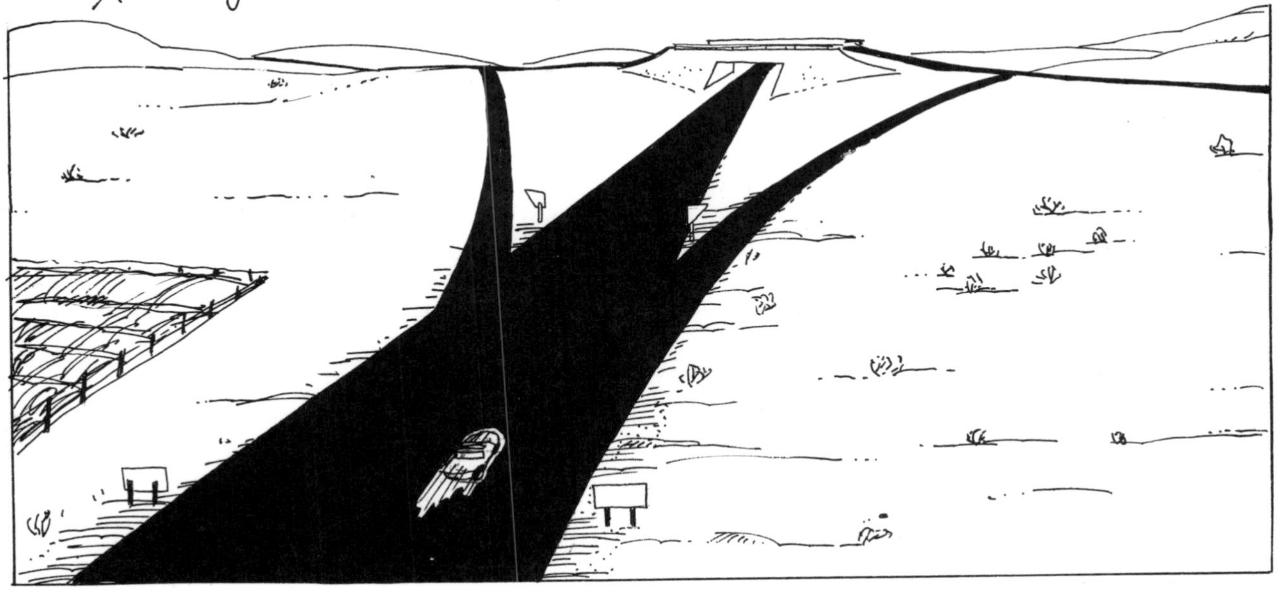

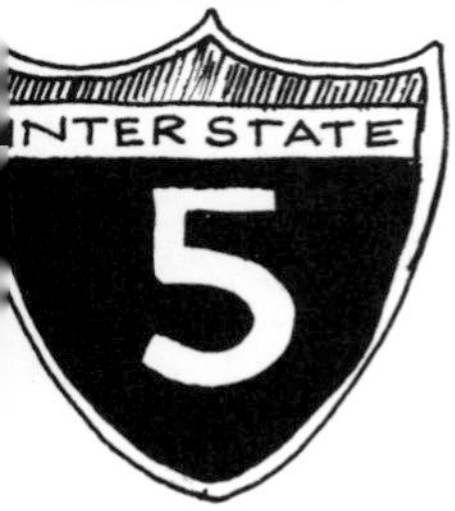
INTER STATE
5

"Candy's Room" on permanent repeat. I'm no fan of the Interstate, but for laying down miles, it's hammer lane all the way, baby.

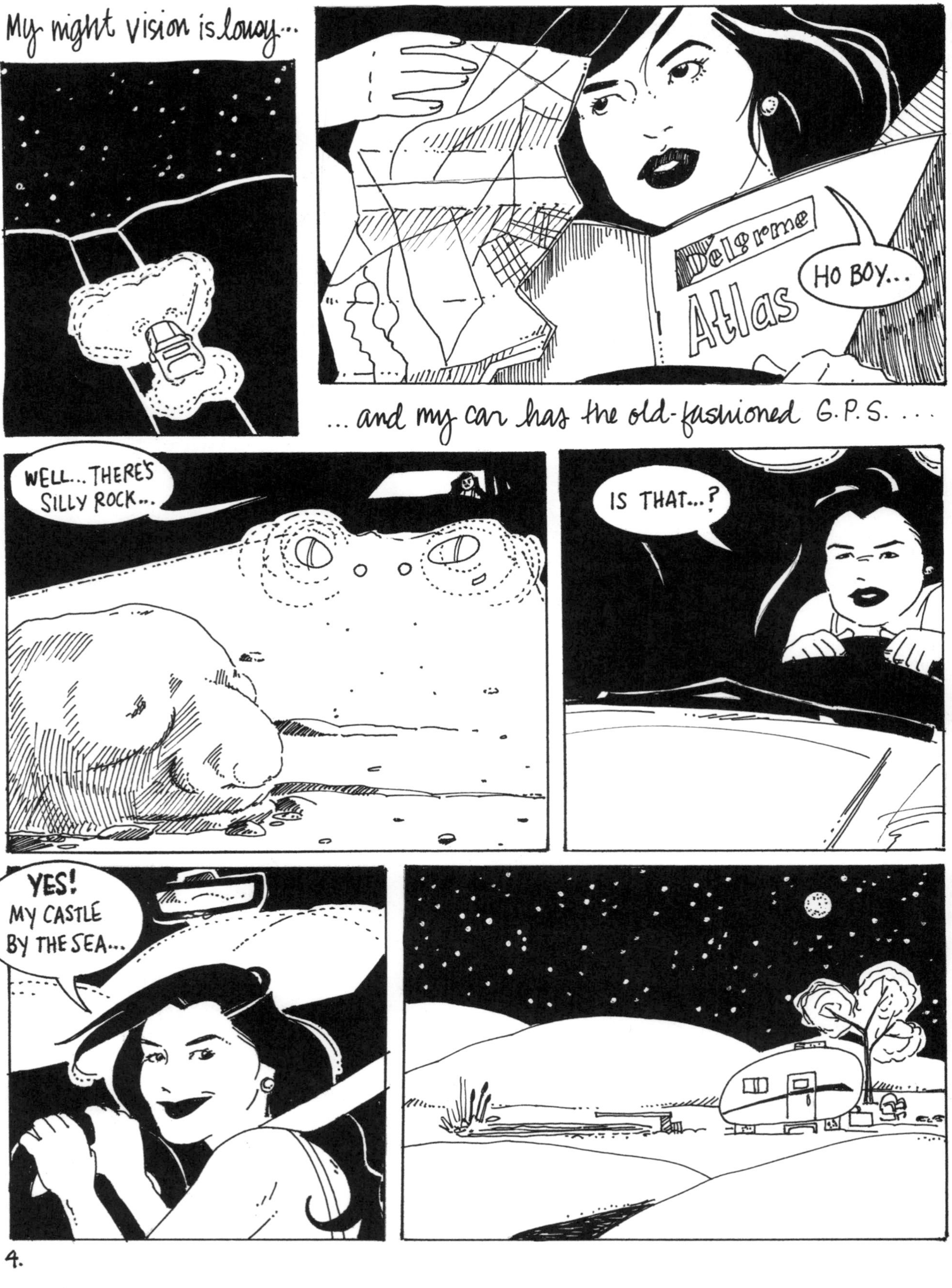
My night vision is lousy...
Delorme Atlas
HO BOY...
...and my car has the old-fashioned G.P.S. ...
WELL...THERE'S SILLY ROCK...
IS THAT...?
YES! MY CASTLE BY THE SEA...

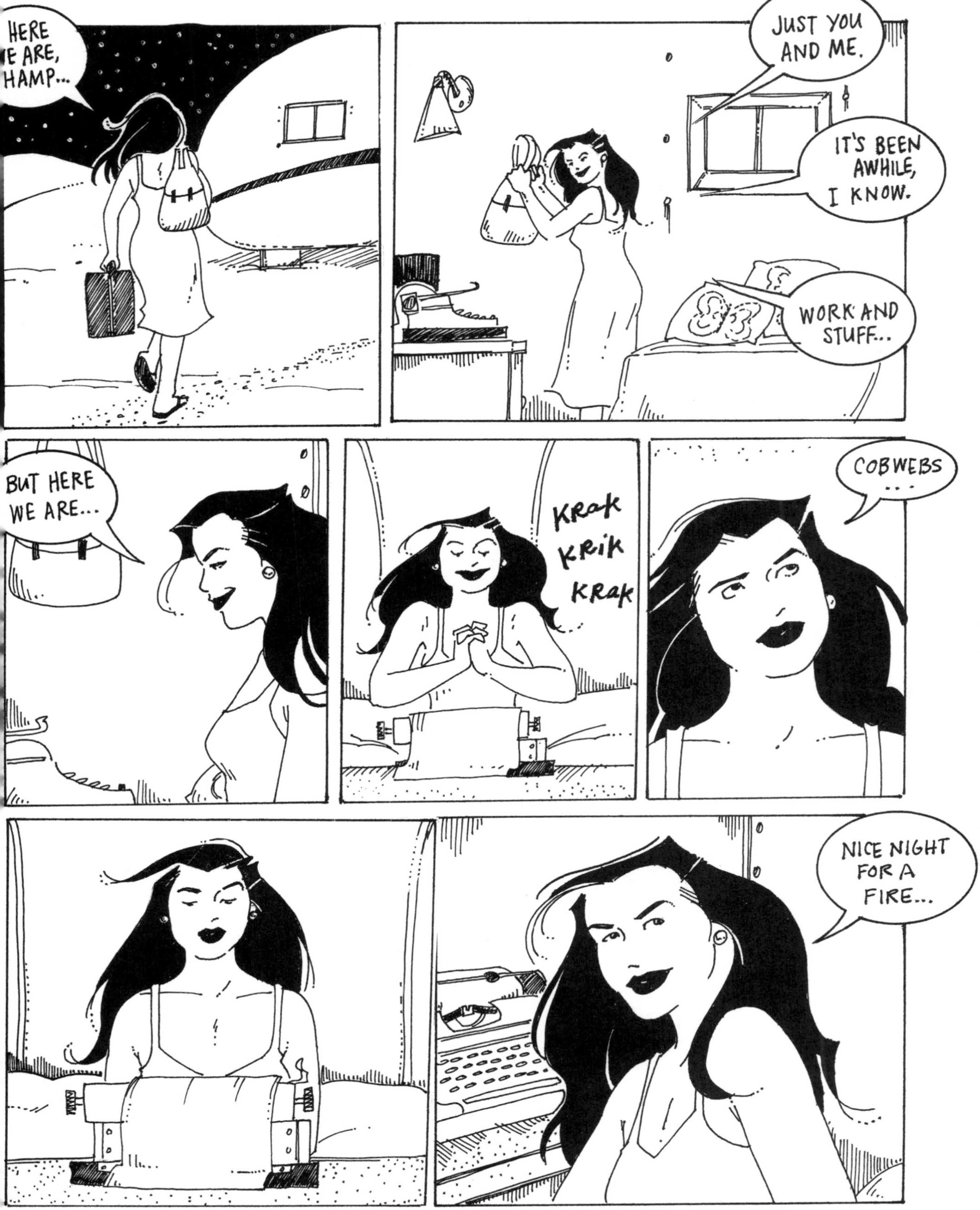
HERE
E ARE,
HAMP...
JUST YOU AND ME.
IT'S BEEN AWHILE, I KNOW.
WORK AND STUFF...
BUT HERE WE ARE...
KRAK
KRIK
KRAK
COBWEBS ...
NICE NIGHT FOR A FIRE...

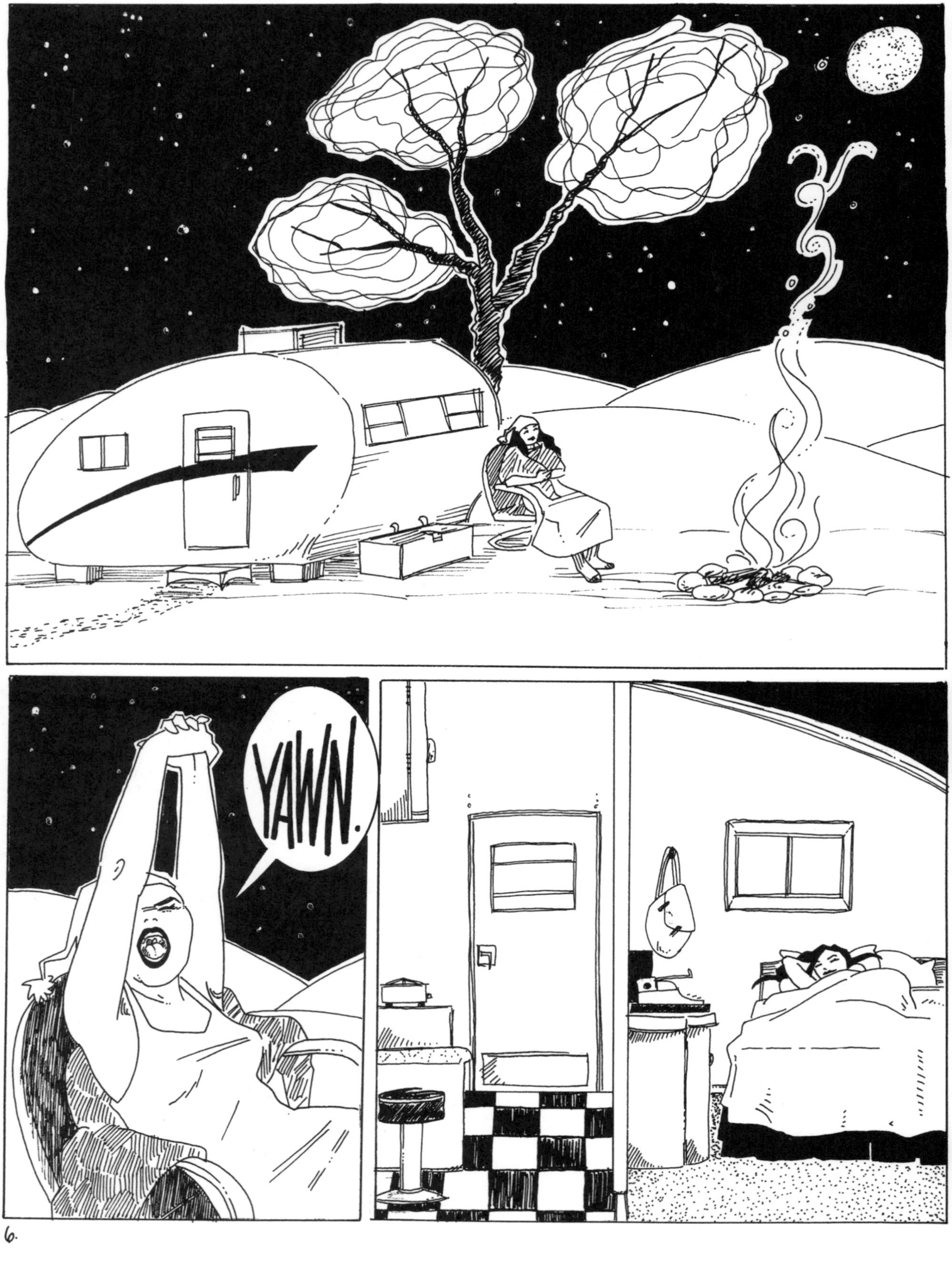
YAWN.

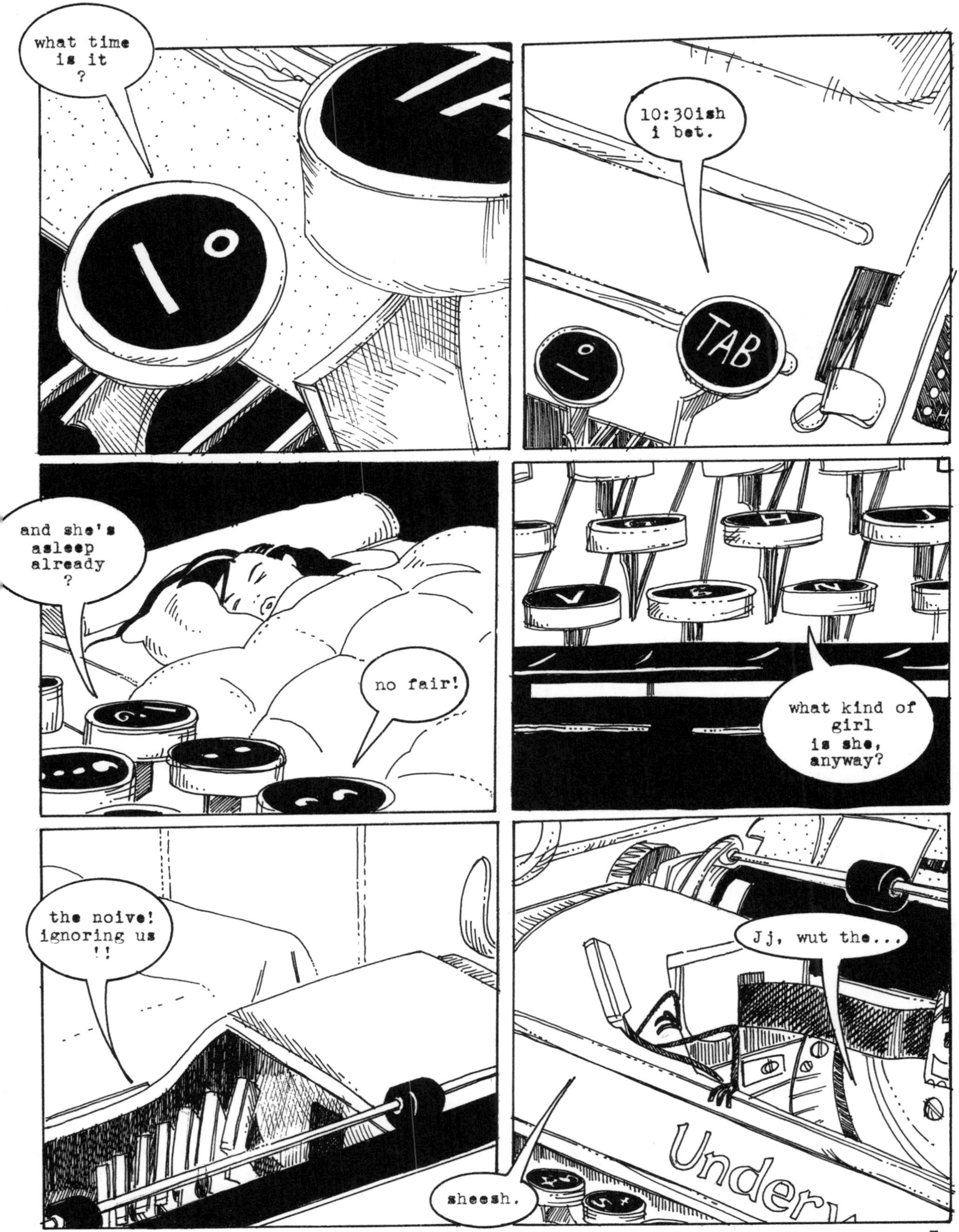
what time is it ?
10:30ish i bet.
TAB
and she's asleep already ?
no fair!
what kind of girl is she, anyway?
the noive! ignoring us !!
Jj, wut the...
sheesh.
Underw

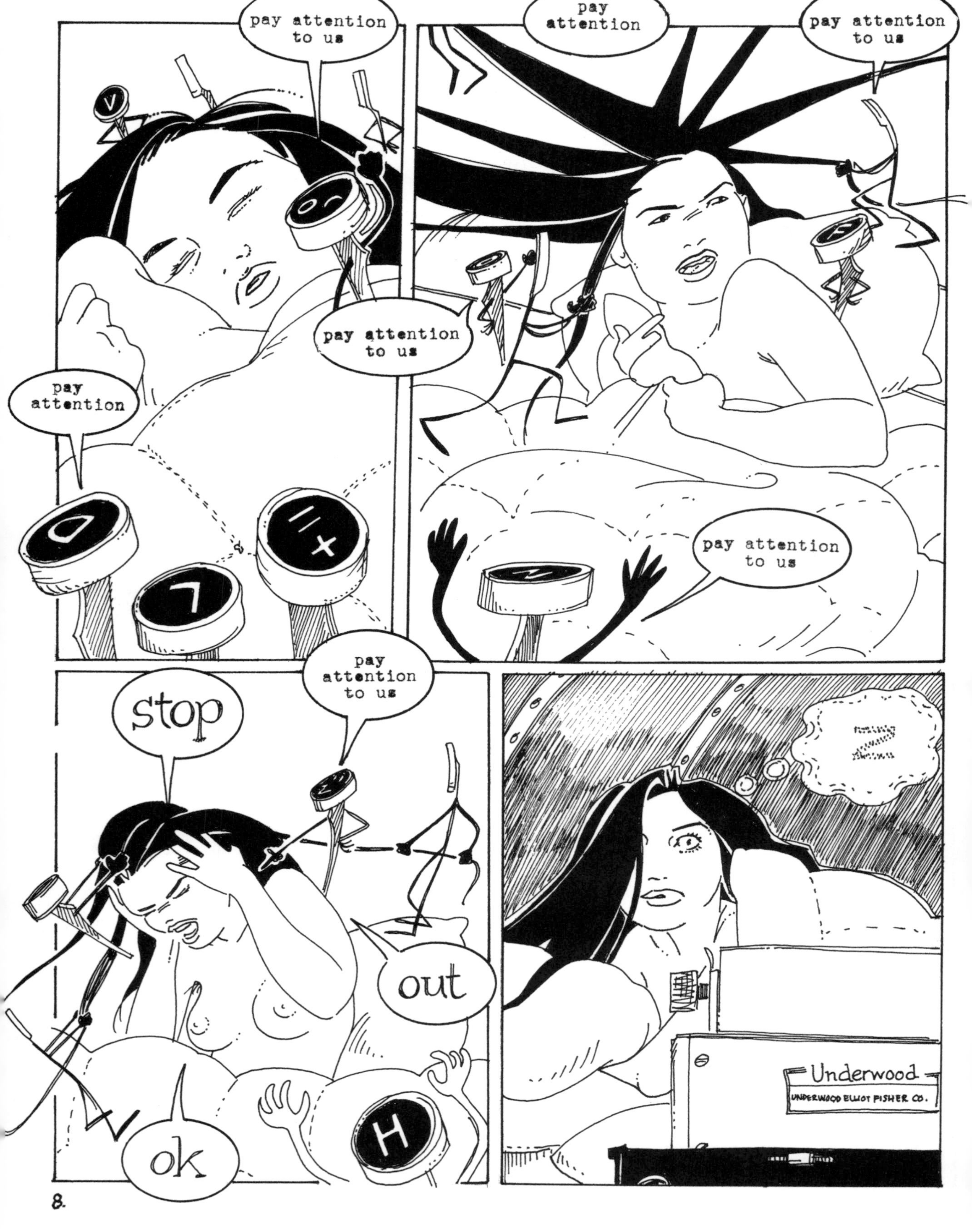
pay attention to us
pay attention to us
pay attention
pay attention
pay attention to us
pay attention to us
pay attention to us
stop
pay attention to us
out
ok
Underwood
UNDERWOOD ELLIOT FISHER CO.

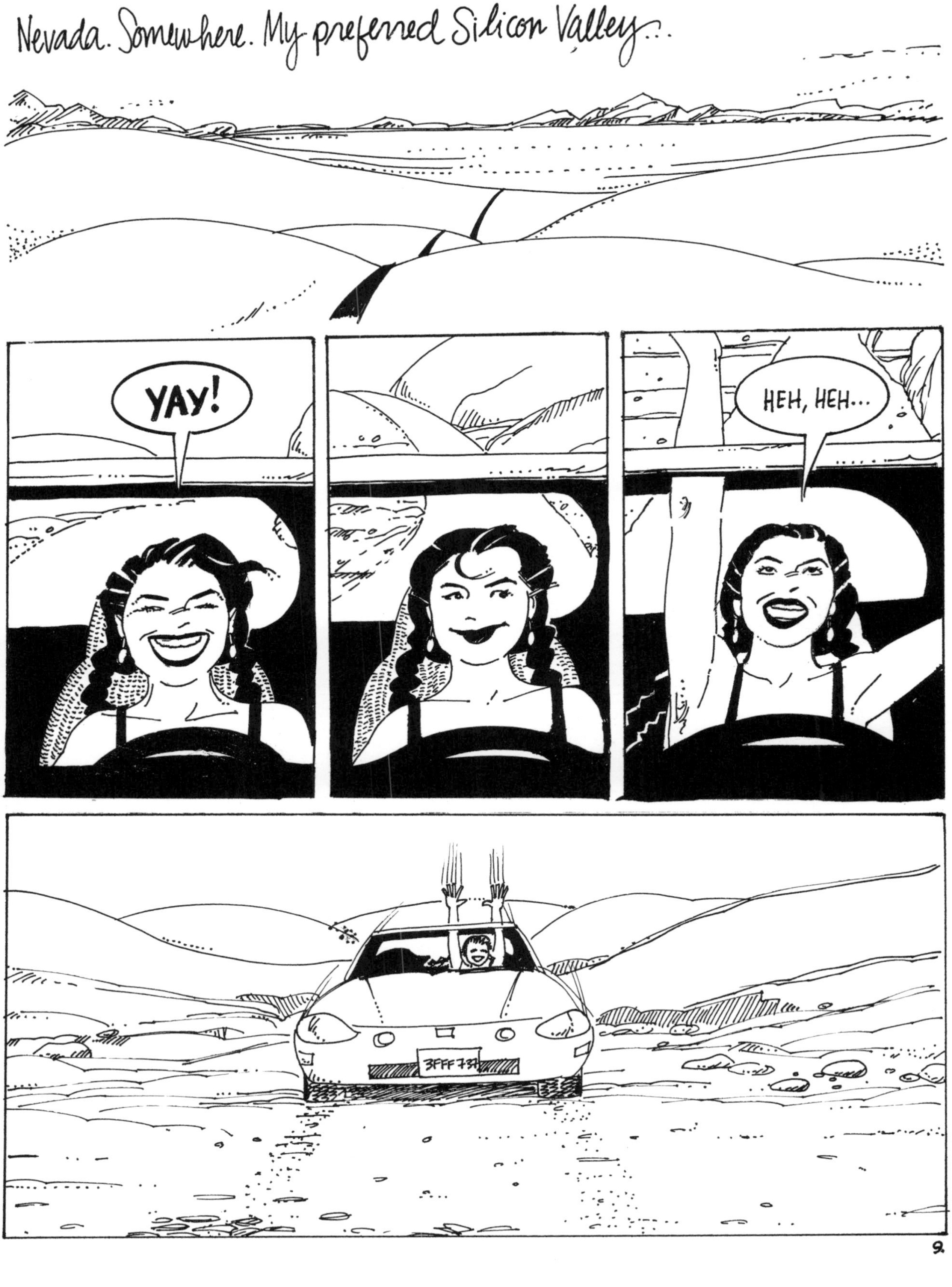
Nevada. Somewhere. My preferred Silicon Valley...
YAY!
HEH, HEH...
3FFF737

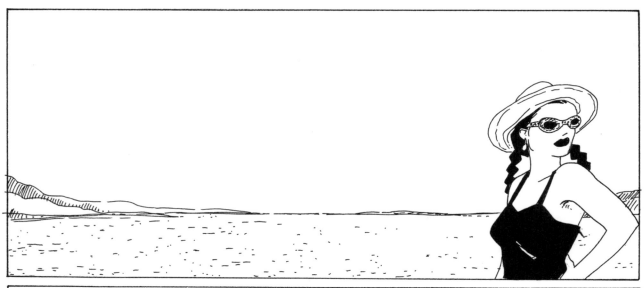

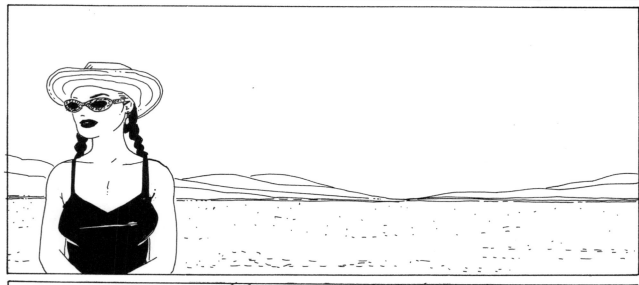

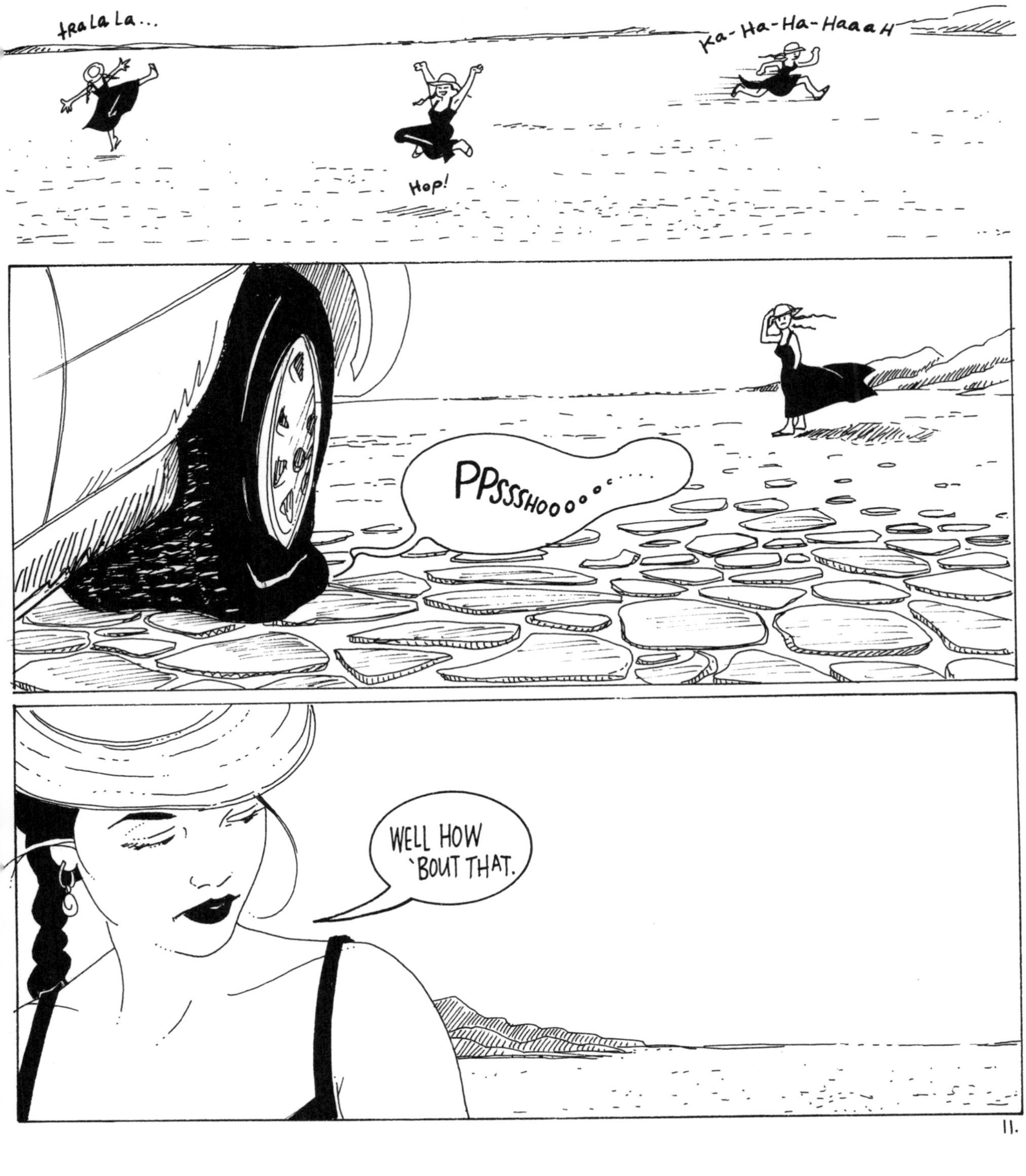
tralala...
Hop!
Ka-Ha-Ha-HaaaH
PPSSSSHOOOoooc.....
WELL HOW 'BOUT THAT.

KRIK KRIK KRIK KR

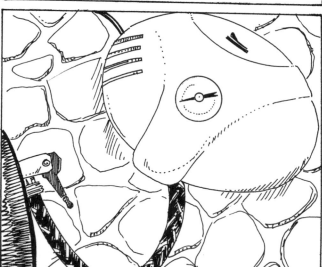

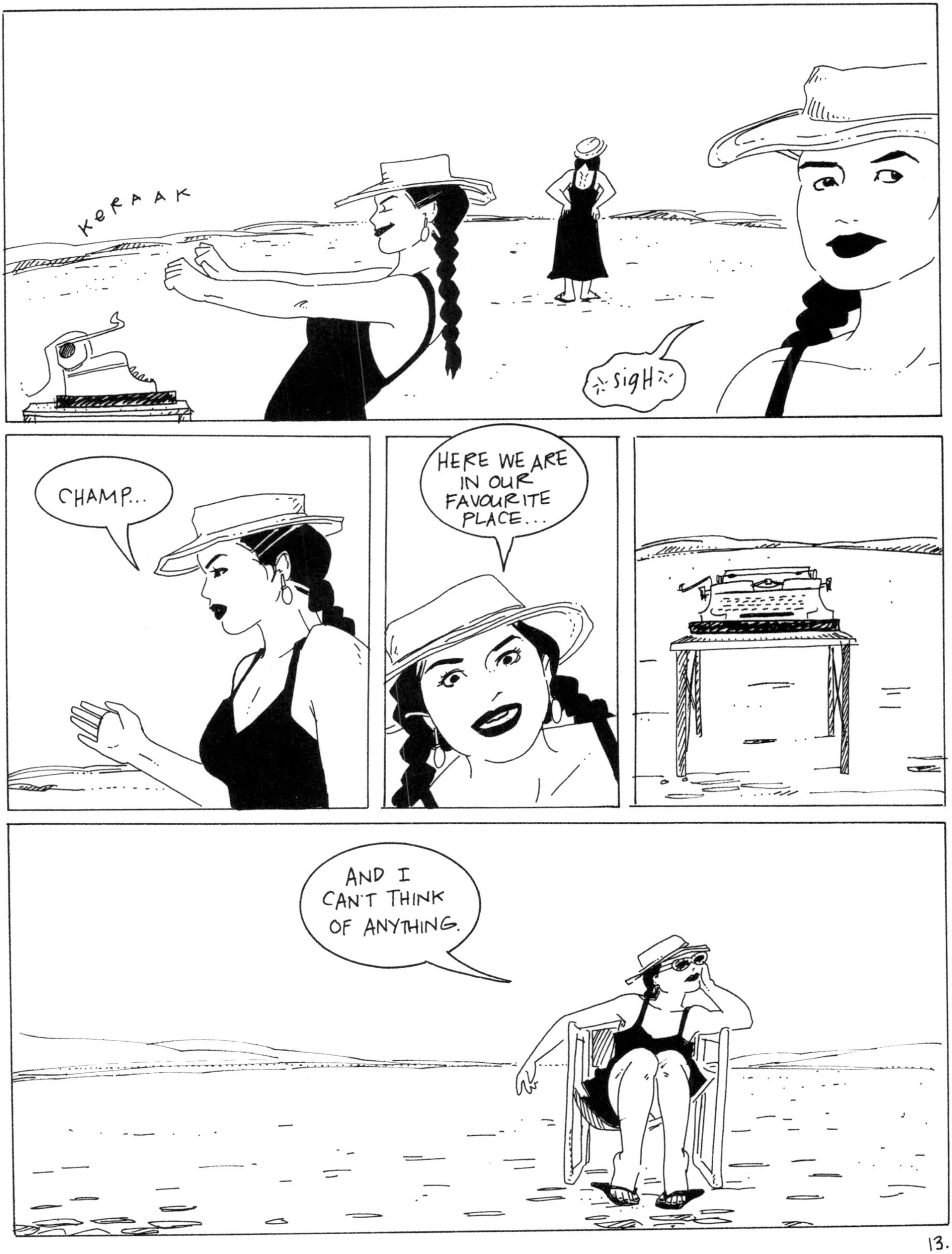
KERAAK
SIGH
CHAMP...
HERE WE ARE IN OUR FAVOURITE PLACE...
AND I CAN'T THINK OF ANYTHING.

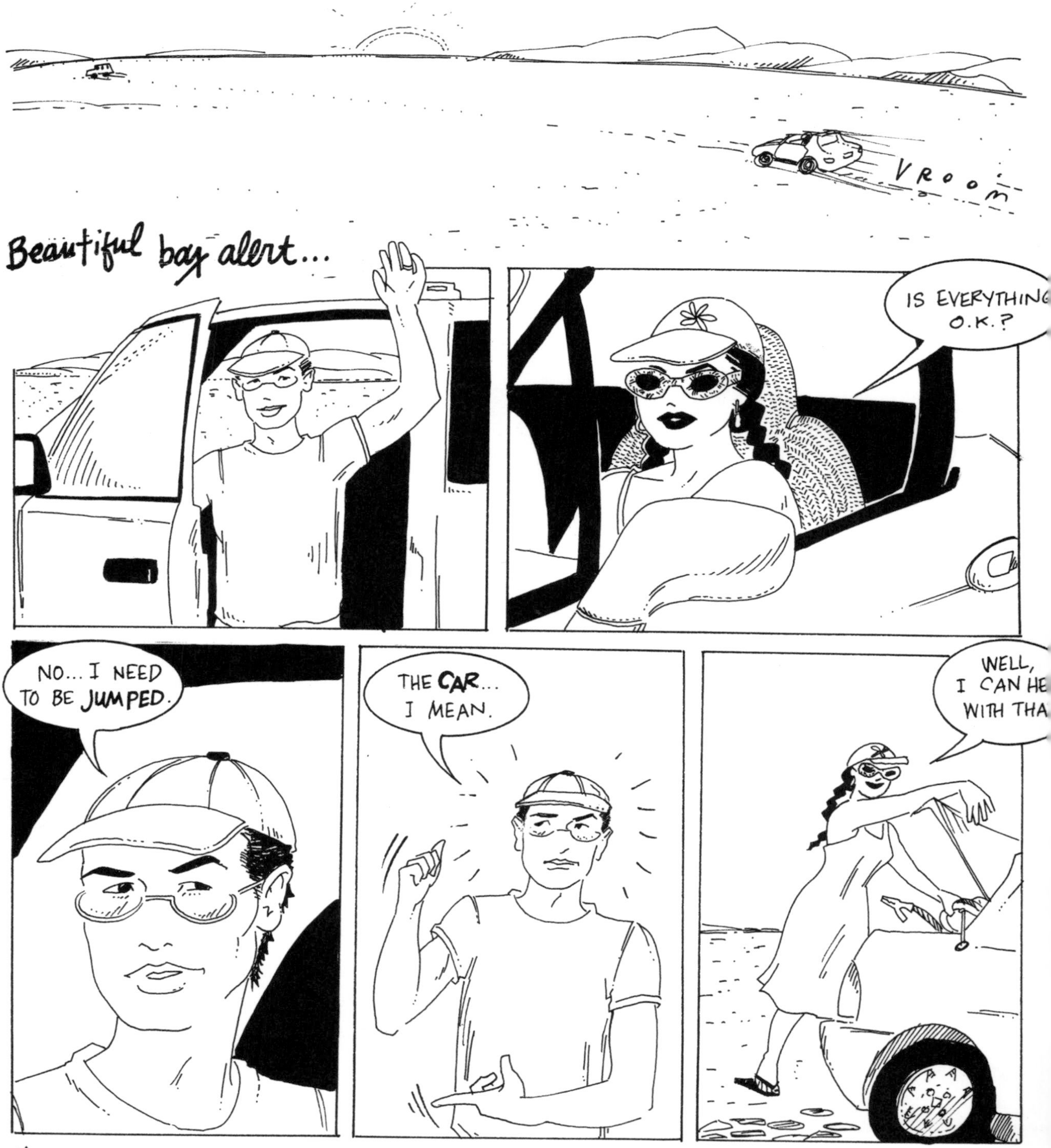
VROOM
Beautiful boy alert...
IS EVERYTHING O.K.?
NO... I NEED TO BE JUMPED.
THE CAR... I MEAN.
WELL, I CAN HE WITH THA

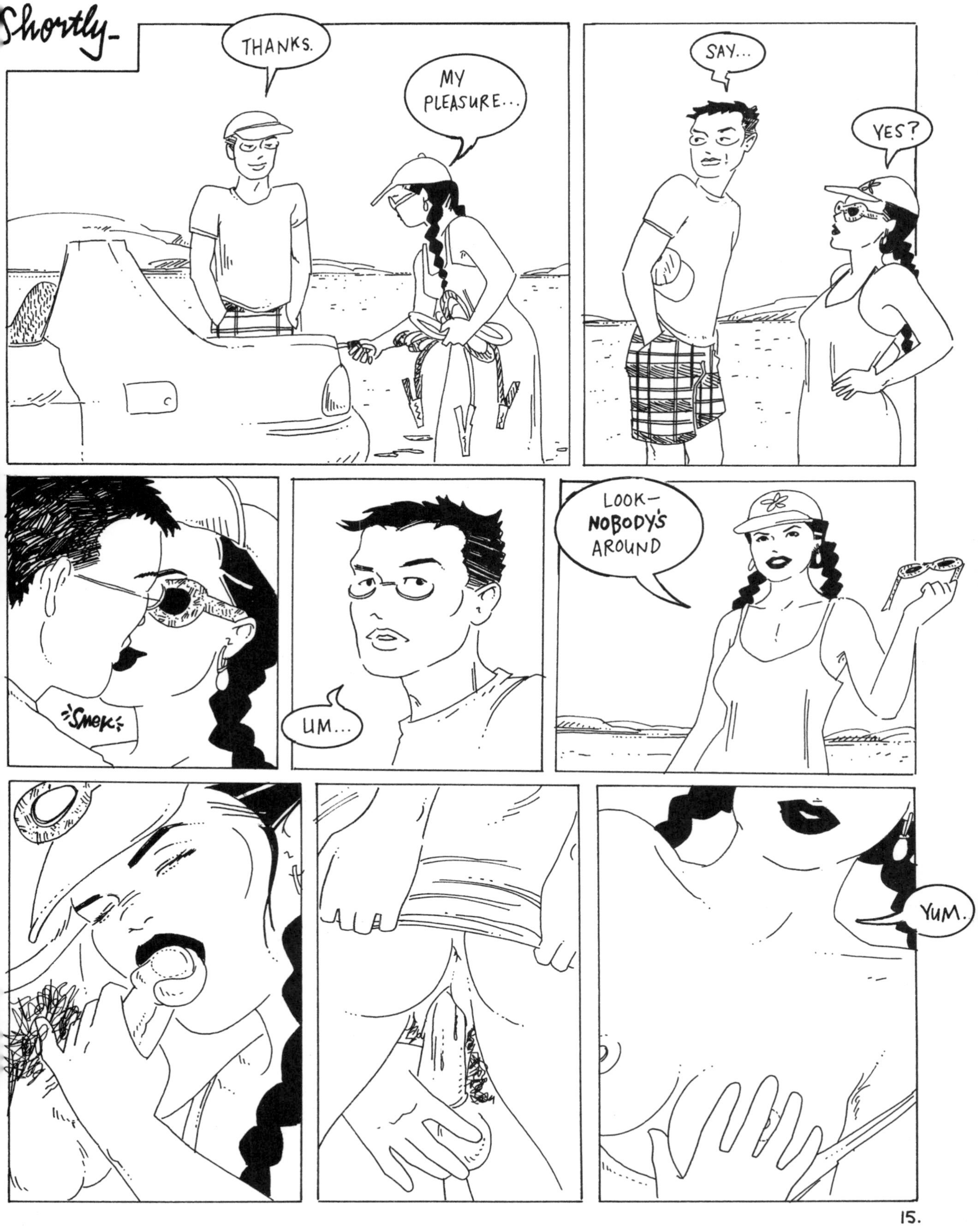
Shortly-
THANKS.
MY PLEASURE...
SAY...
YES?
SMEK
UM...
LOOK— NOBODY'S AROUND
YUM.

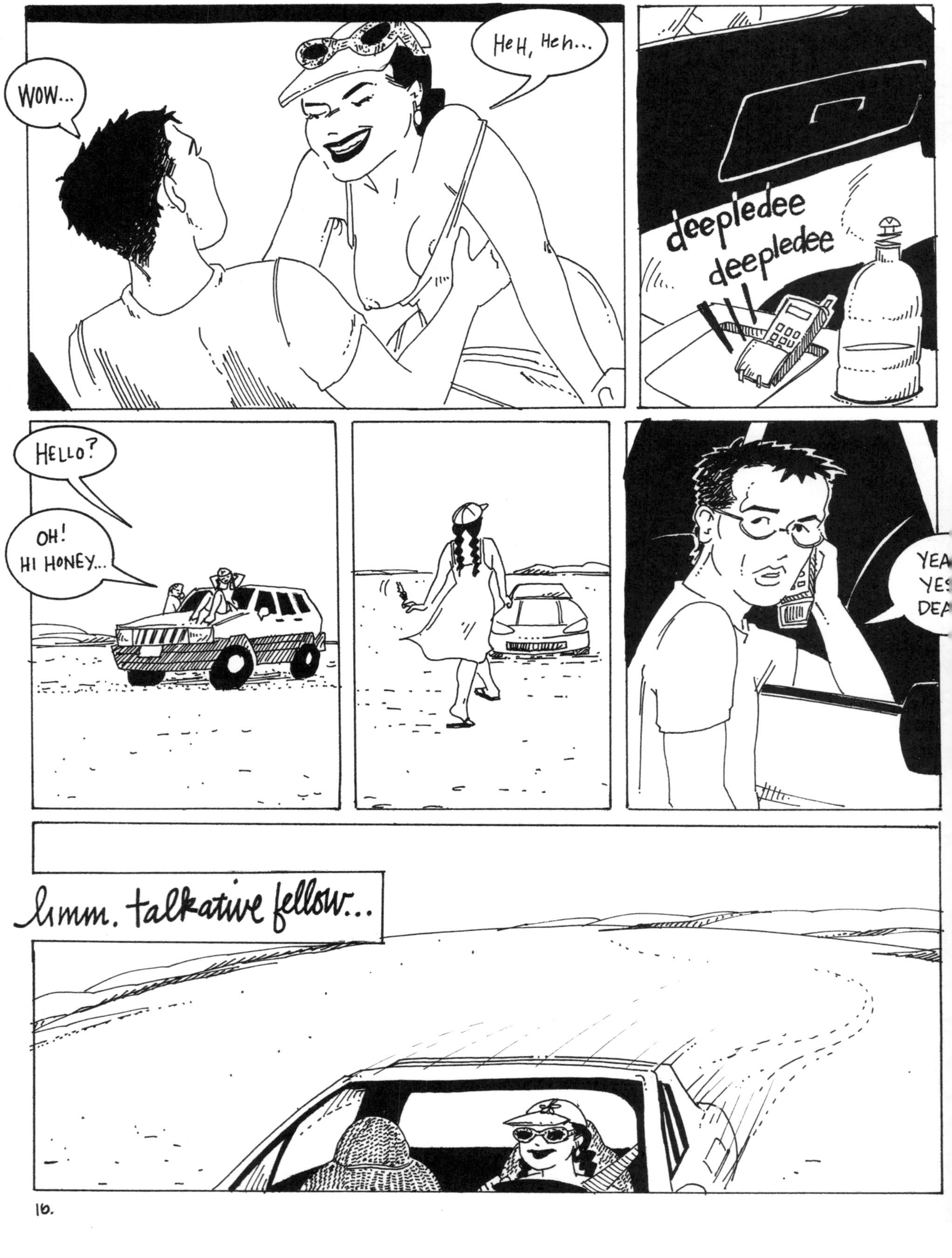
WOW...
HEH, HEH...
deepledee
deepledee
HELLO?
OH!
HI HONEY...
hmm. talkative fellow...

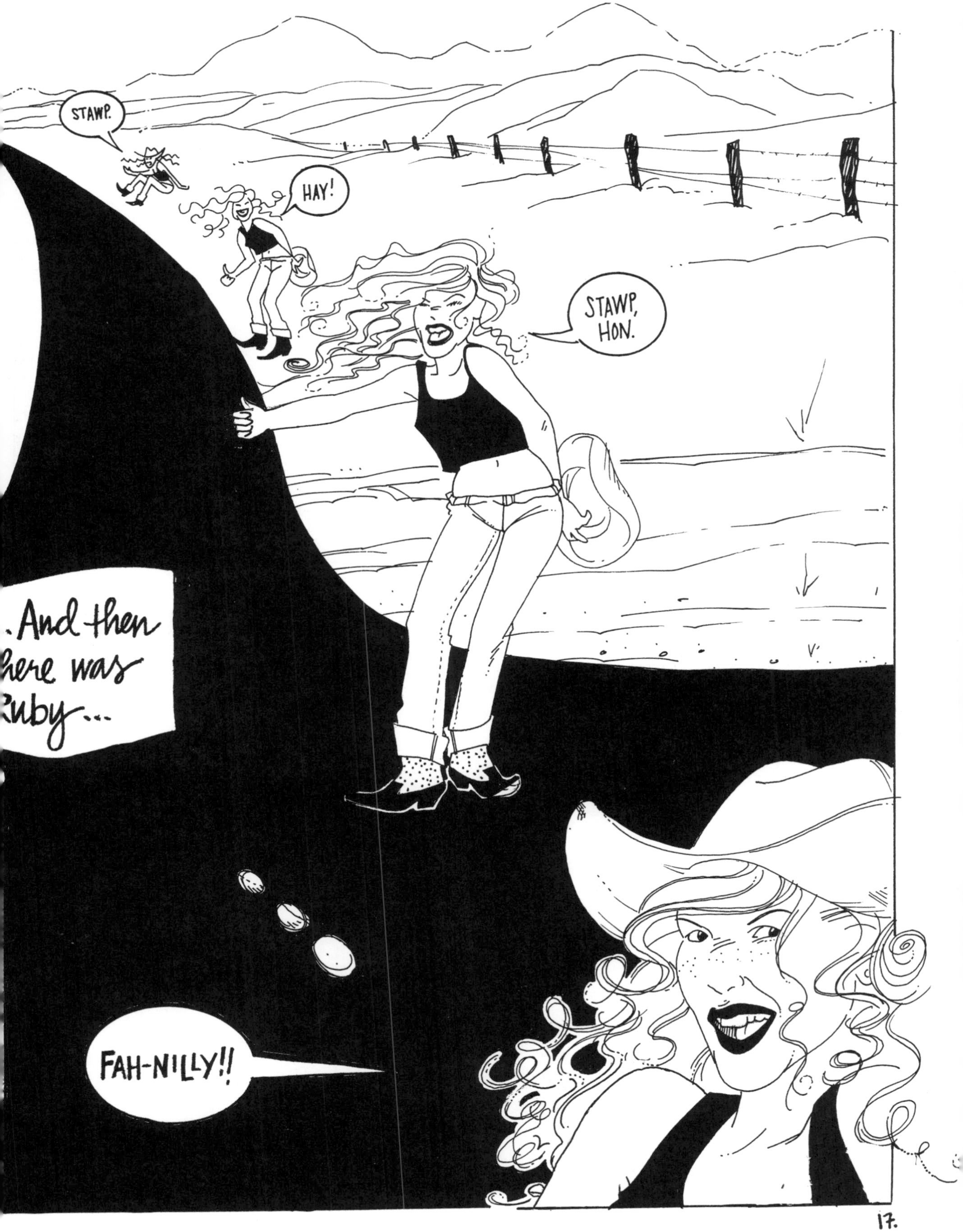

STAWP.
HAY!
STAWP, HON.
. And then here was Ruby...
FAH-NILLY!!

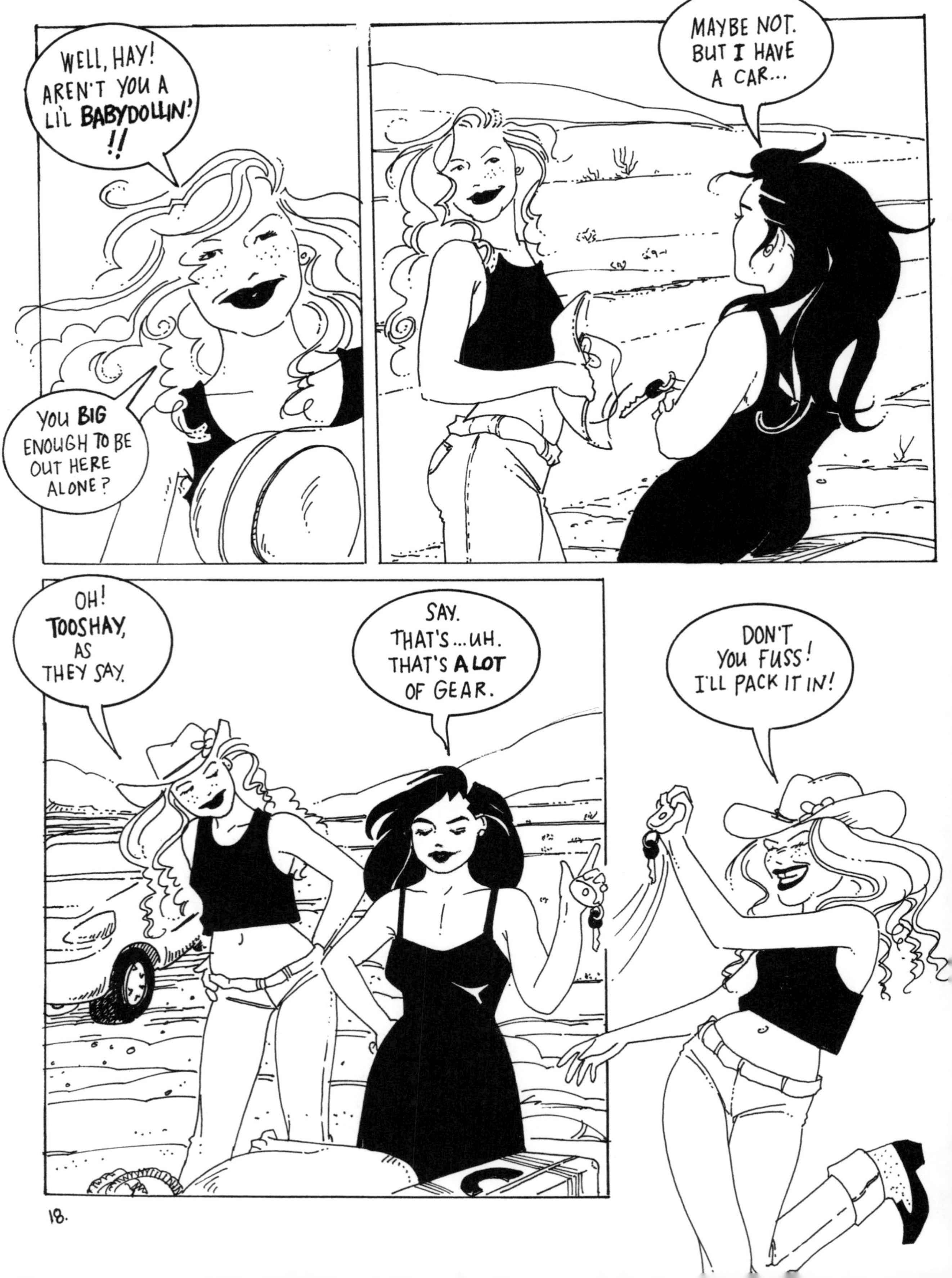
WELL, HAY! AREN'T YOU A LI'L **BABYDOLLIN'** !!
YOU **BIG** ENOUGH **TO** BE OUT HERE ALONE?
MAYBE NOT. BUT **I** HAVE A CAR...
OH! **TOOSHAY,** AS THEY SAY.
SAY. THAT'S...UH. THAT'S **A LOT** OF GEAR.
DON'T YOU FUSS! I'LL PACK IT IN!

Ruby was just too much... too much big yellow hair... too much redsmacking lipstick. Her legs were too long, her voice too loud and crazy like a cartoon character...

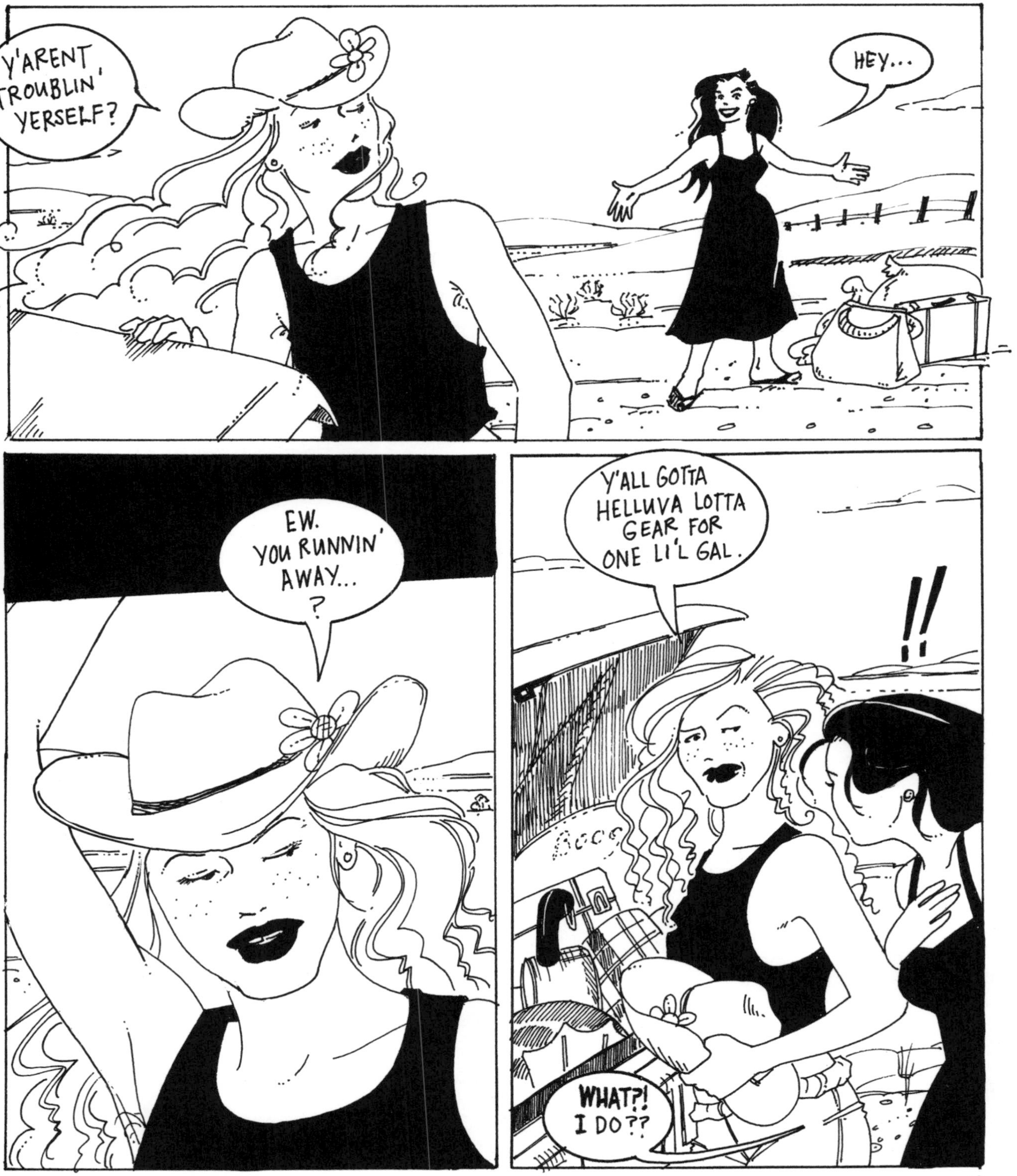
Y'ARENT TROUBLIN' YERSELF?
HEY...
EW. YOU RUNNIN' AWAY... ?
Y'ALL GOTTA HELLUVA LOTTA GEAR FOR ONE LI'L GAL.
!!
WHAT?! I DO??

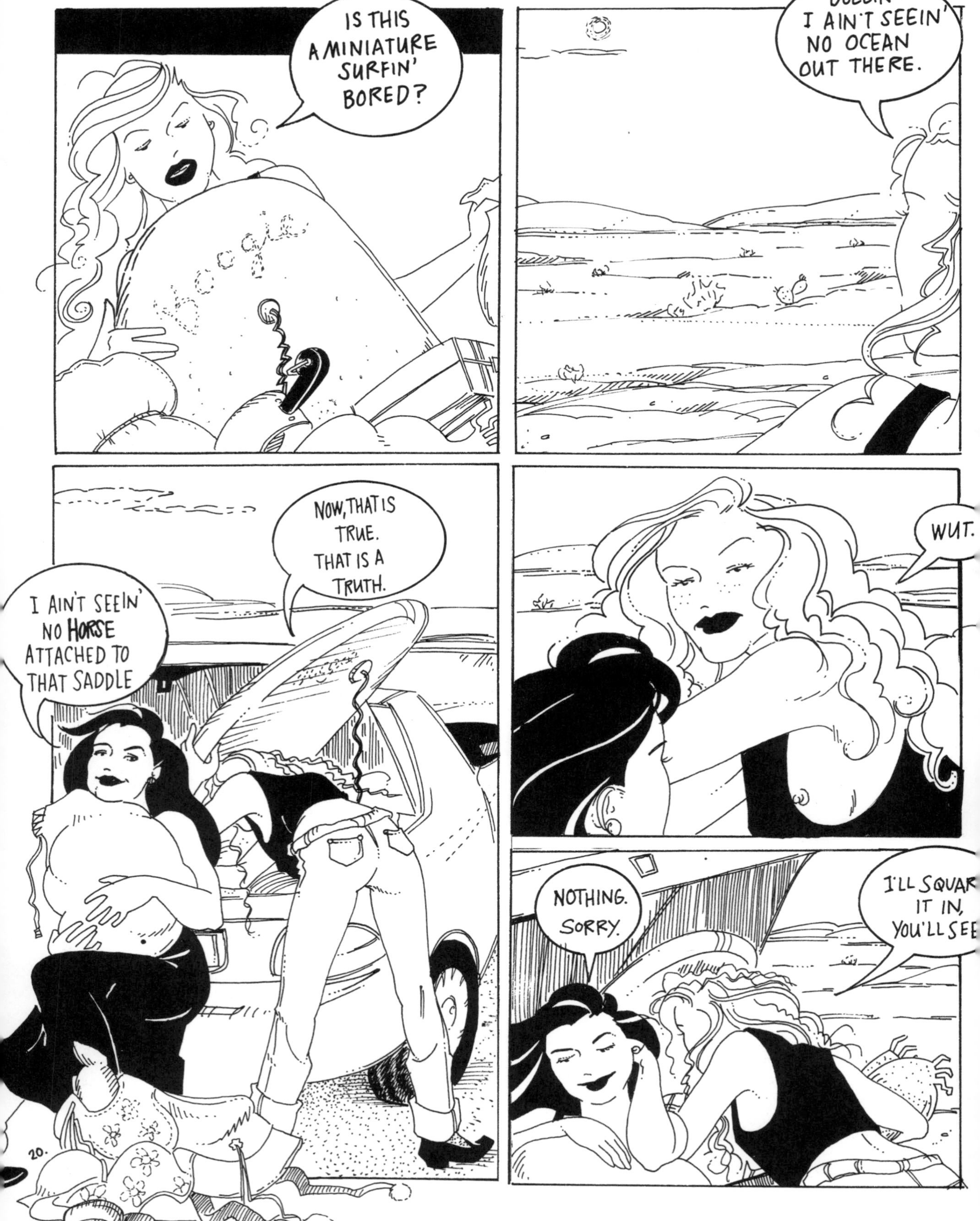
IS THIS A MINIATURE SURFIN' BORED?
DOLLIN' I AIN'T SEEIN' NO OCEAN OUT THERE.
NOW, THAT IS TRUE. THAT IS A TRUTH.
I AIN'T SEEIN' NO HORSE ATTACHED TO THAT SADDLE
WUT.
NOTHING. SORRY.
I'LL SQUAR IT IN, YOU'LL SEE

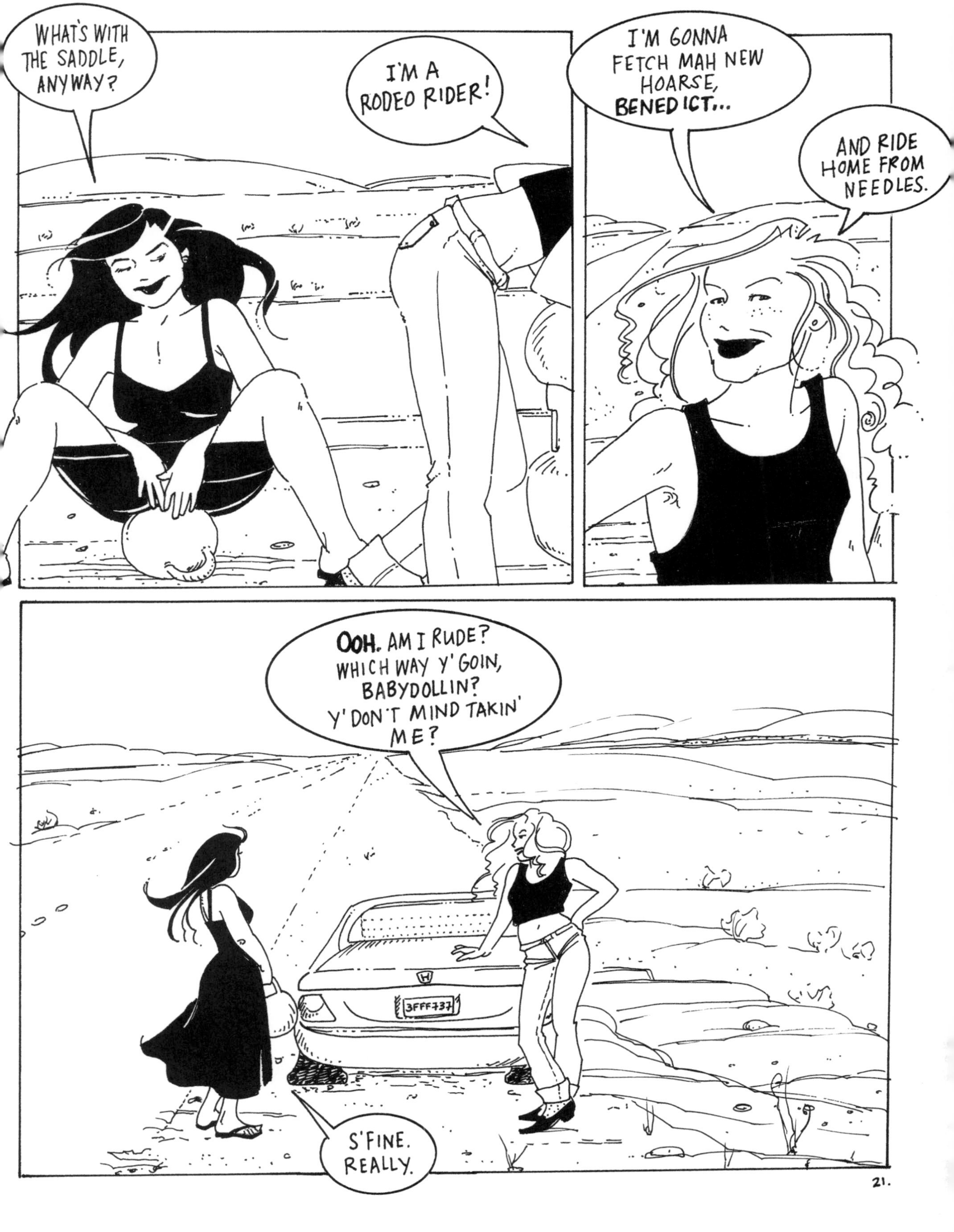
WHAT'S WITH THE SADDLE, ANYWAY?
I'M A RODEO RIDER!
I'M GONNA FETCH MAH NEW HOARSE, BENEDICT...
AND RIDE HOME FROM NEEDLES.
OOH. AM I RUDE? WHICH WAY Y' GOIN, BABYDOLLIN? Y' DON'T MIND TAKIN' ME?
S'FINE. REALLY.
3FFF737

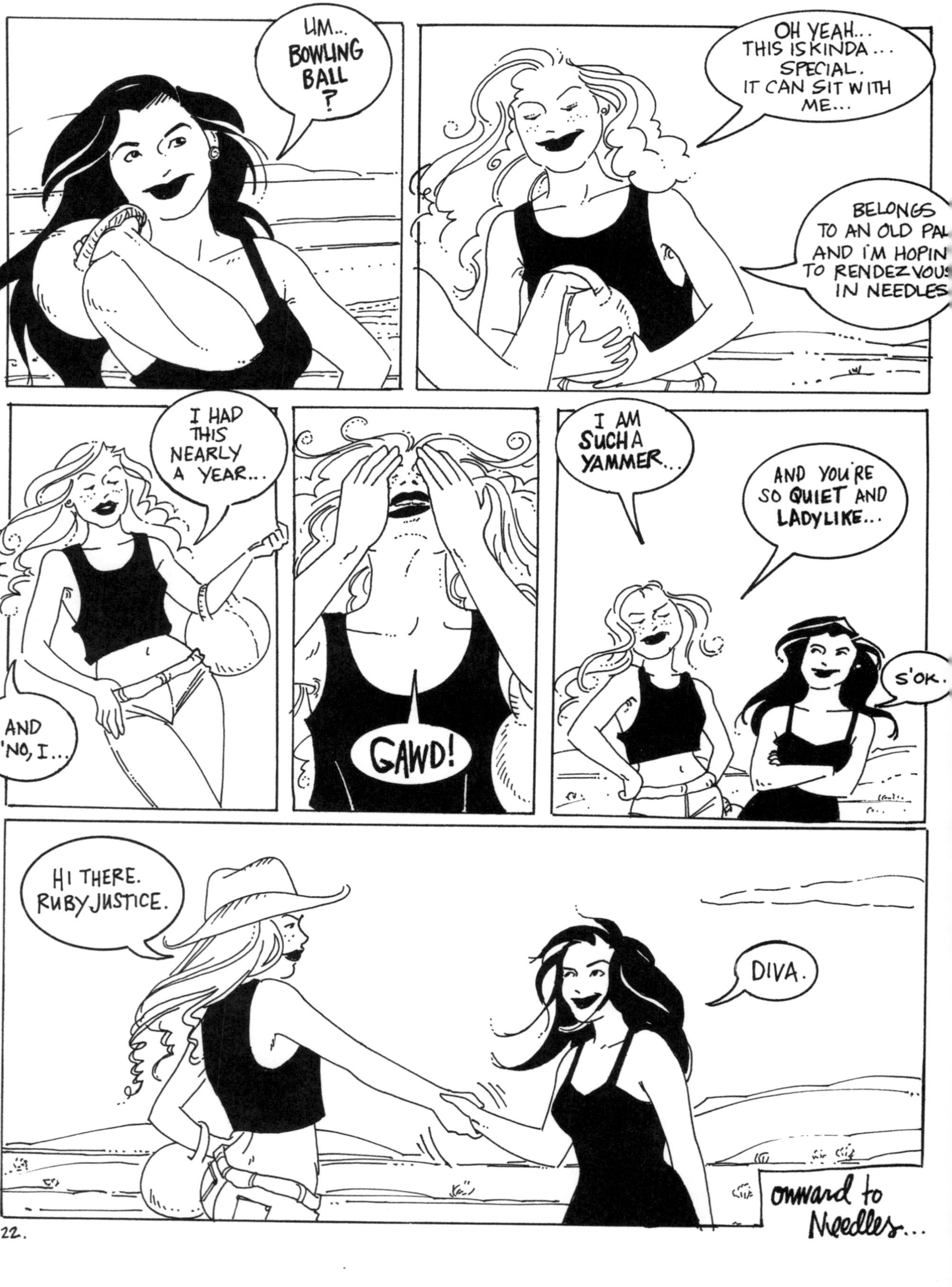

UM... BOWLING BALL ?
OH YEAH... THIS IS KINDA... SPECIAL. IT CAN SIT WITH ME...
BELONGS TO AN OLD PAL AND I'M HOPIN TO RENDEZVOUS IN NEEDLES
I HAD THIS NEARLY A YEAR...
AND Y'NO, I...
GAWD!
I AM SUCH A YAMMER...
AND YOU'RE SO QUIET AND LADYLIKE...
S'OK.
HI THERE. RUBY JUSTICE.
DIVA.
onward to Needles...

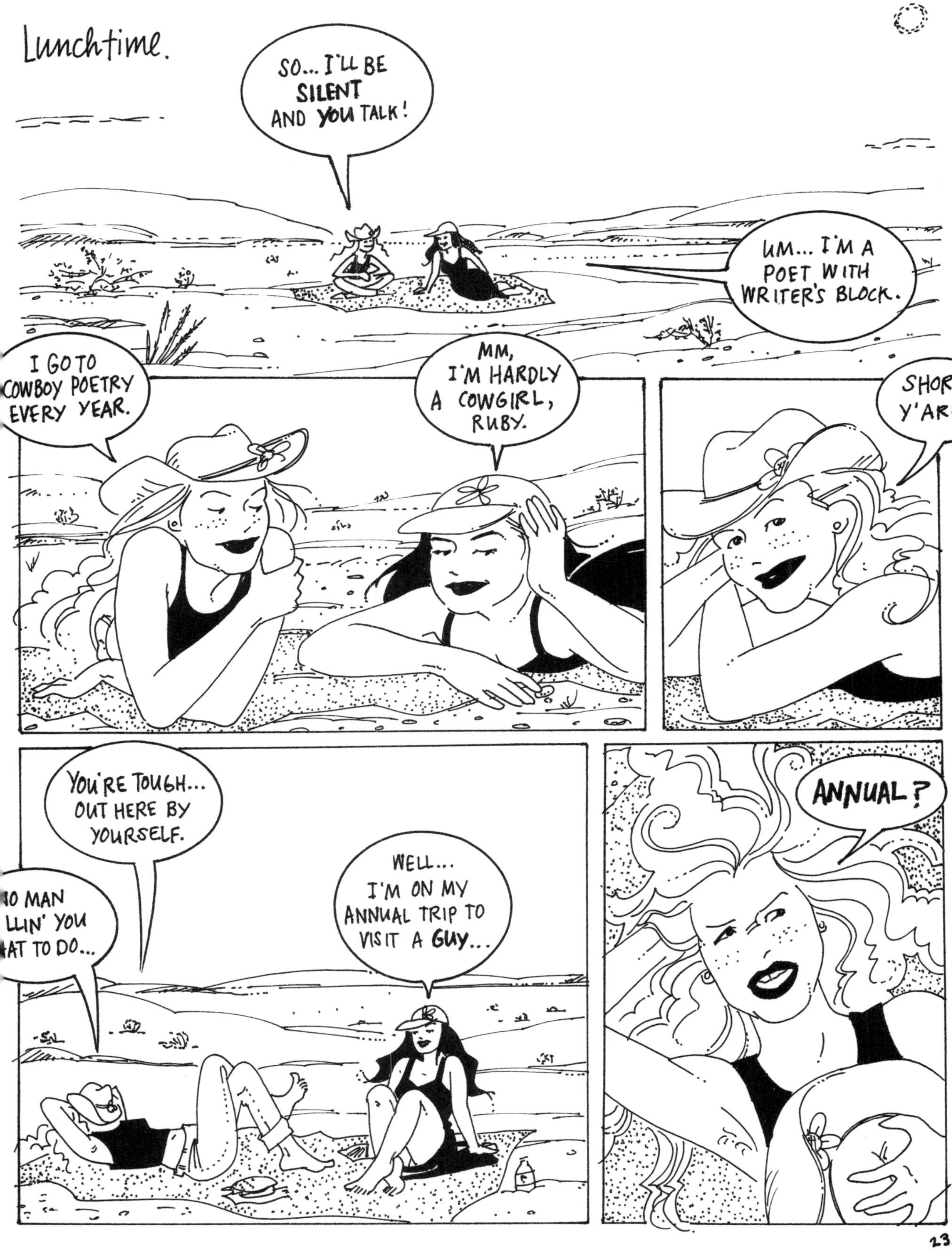

Lunchtime.
SO... I'LL BE SILENT AND YOU TALK!
UM... I'M A POET WITH WRITER'S BLOCK.
I GO TO COWBOY POETRY EVERY YEAR.
MM, I'M HARDLY A COWGIRL, RUBY.
SHORE Y'ARE!
YOU'RE TOUGH... OUT HERE BY YOURSELF.
O MAN LLIN' YOU AT TO DO...
WELL... I'M ON MY ANNUAL TRIP TO VISIT A GUY...
ANNUAL?

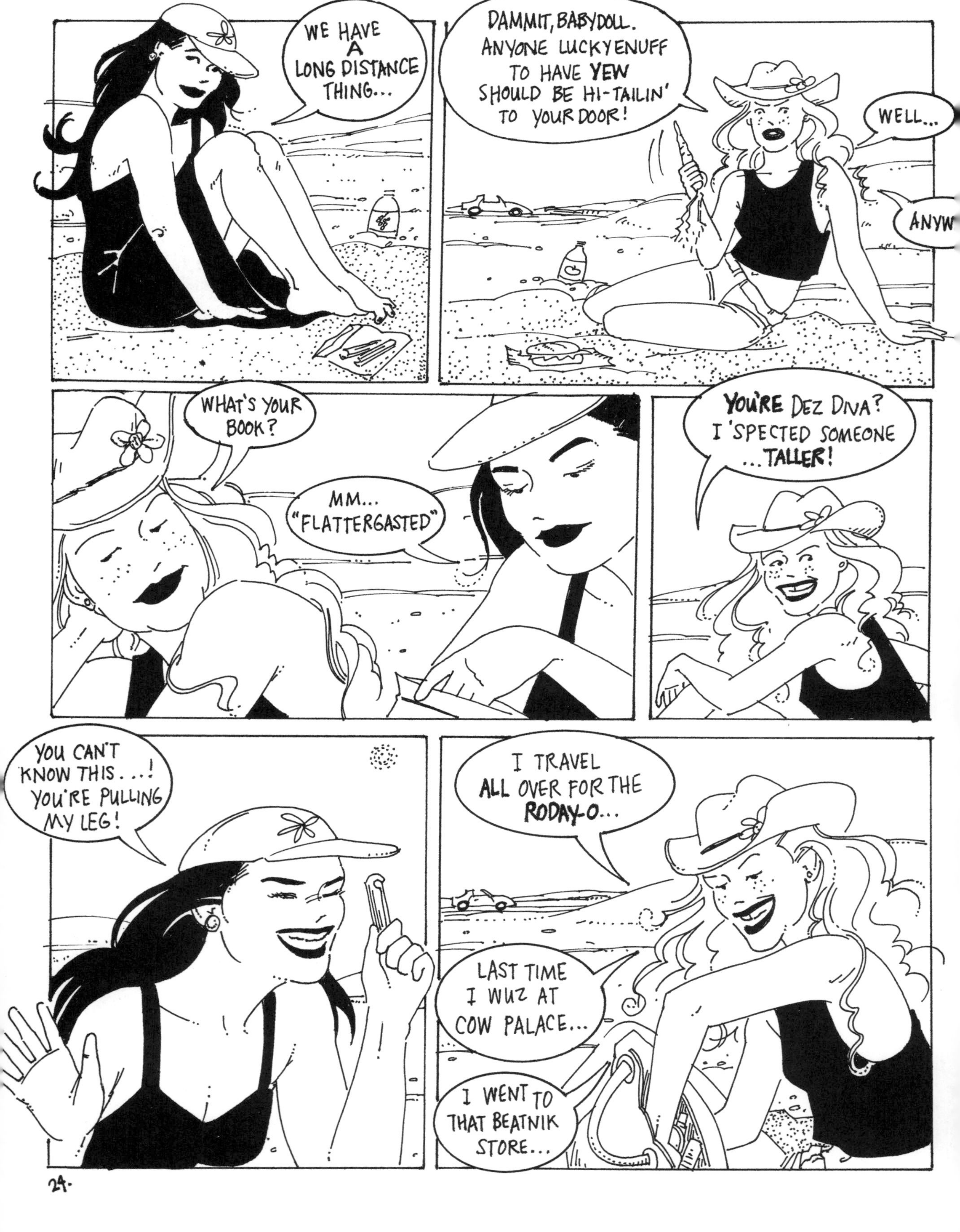
WE HAVE A LONG DISTANCE THING...
DAMMIT, BABYDOLL. ANYONE LUCKYENUFF TO HAVE YEW SHOULD BE HI-TAILIN' TO YOUR DOOR!
WELL...
ANYW
WHAT'S YOUR BOOK?
MM... "FLATTERGASTED"
YOU'RE DEZ DIVA? I 'SPECTED SOMEONE ...TALLER!
YOU CAN'T KNOW THIS...! YOU'RE PULLING MY LEG!
I TRAVEL ALL OVER FOR THE RODAY-O...
LAST TIME I WUZ AT COW PALACE...
I WENT TO THAT BEATNIK STORE...

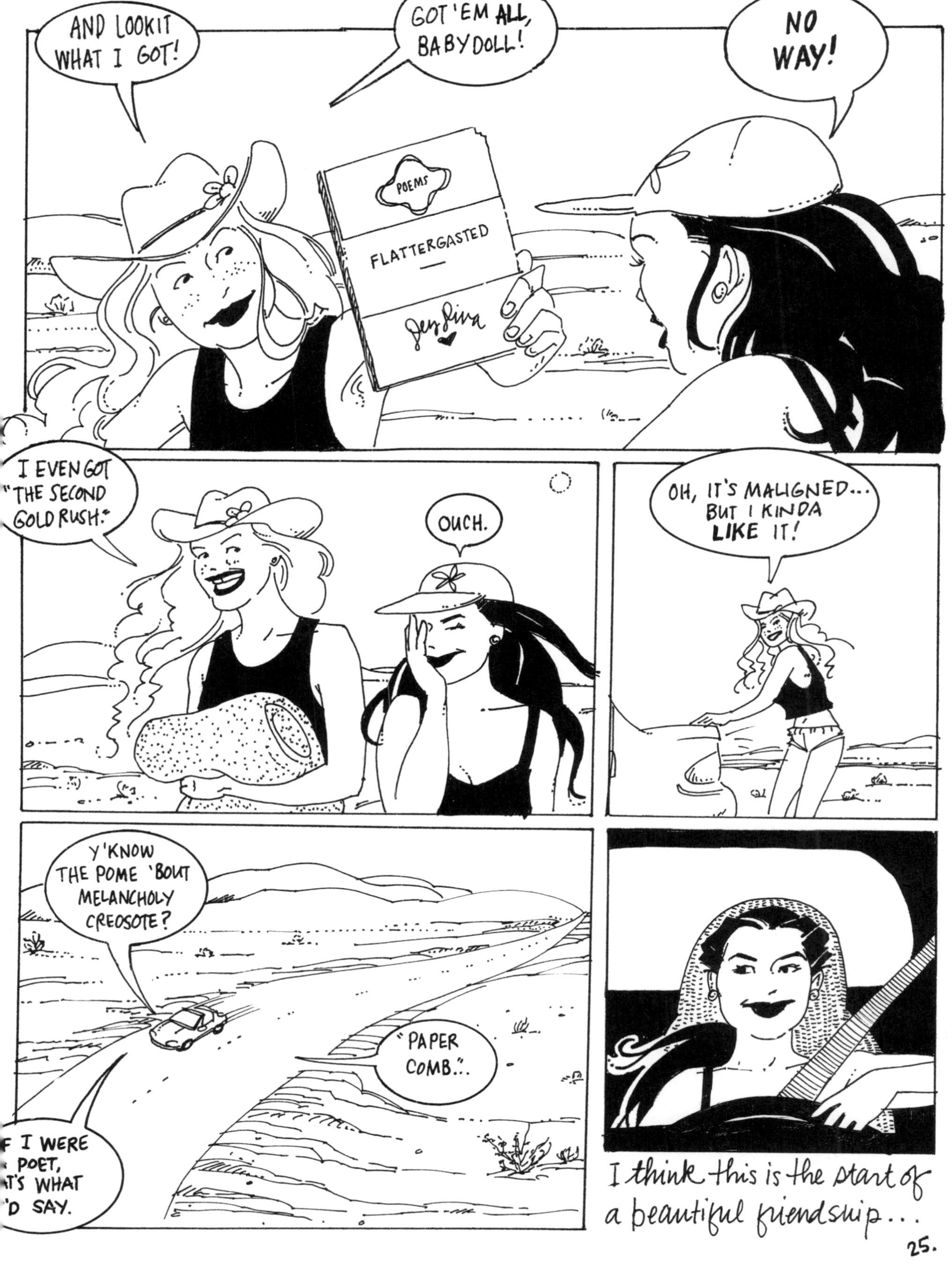
AND LOOKIT WHAT I GOT!
GOT 'EM ALL, BABYDOLL!
NO WAY!
POEMS
FLATTERGASTED
I EVEN GOT "THE SECOND GOLD RUSH."
OUCH.
OH, IT'S MALIGNED... BUT I KINDA LIKE IT!
Y'KNOW THE POME 'BOUT MELANCHOLY CREOSOTE?
"PAPER COMB."...
I think this is the start of a beautiful friendship...

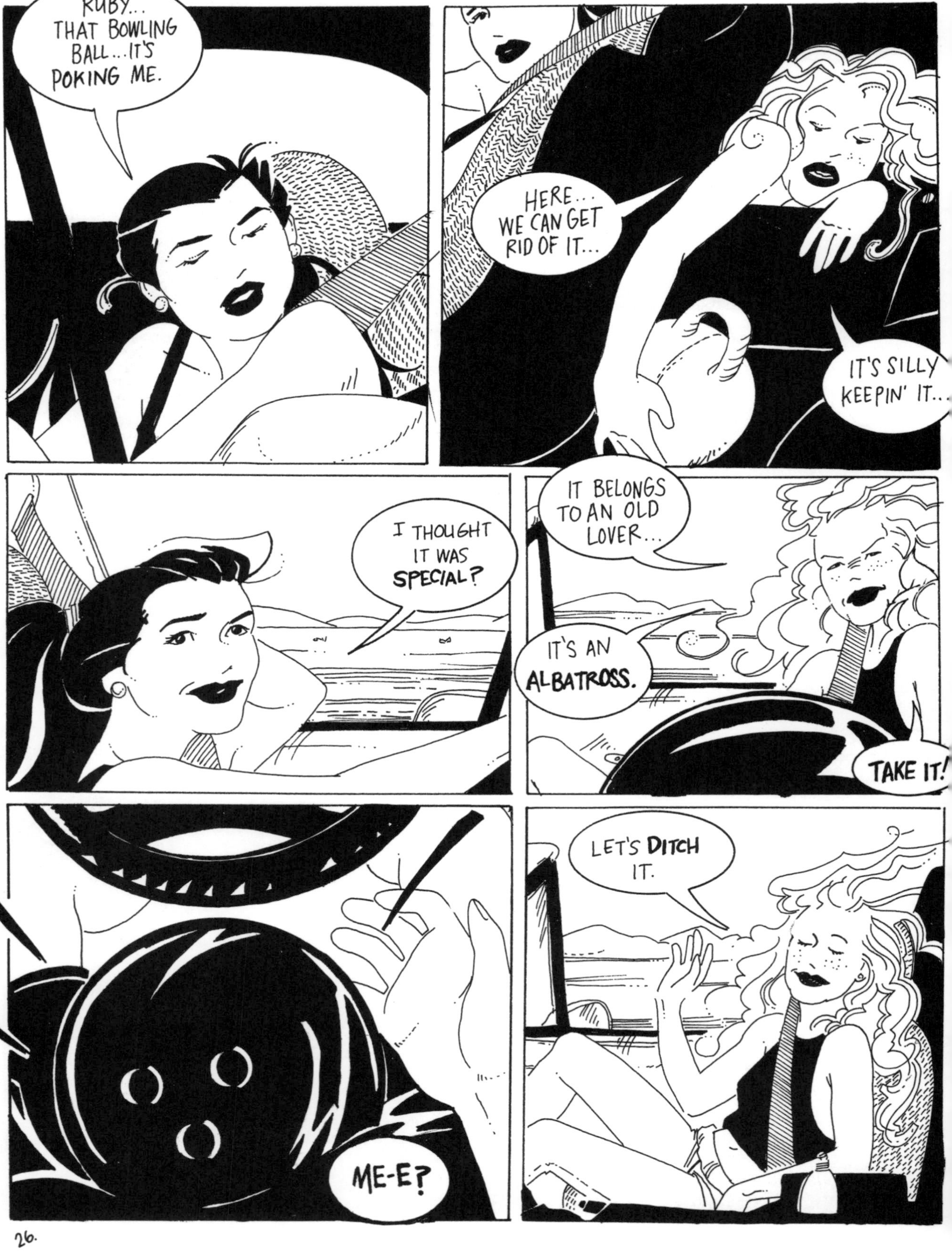
RUBY... THAT BOWLING BALL...IT'S POKING ME.
HERE... WE CAN GET RID OF IT...
IT'S SILLY KEEPIN' IT...
I THOUGHT IT WAS SPECIAL?
IT BELONGS TO AN OLD LOVER...
IT'S AN ALBATROSS.
TAKE IT!
ME-E?
LET'S DITCH IT.

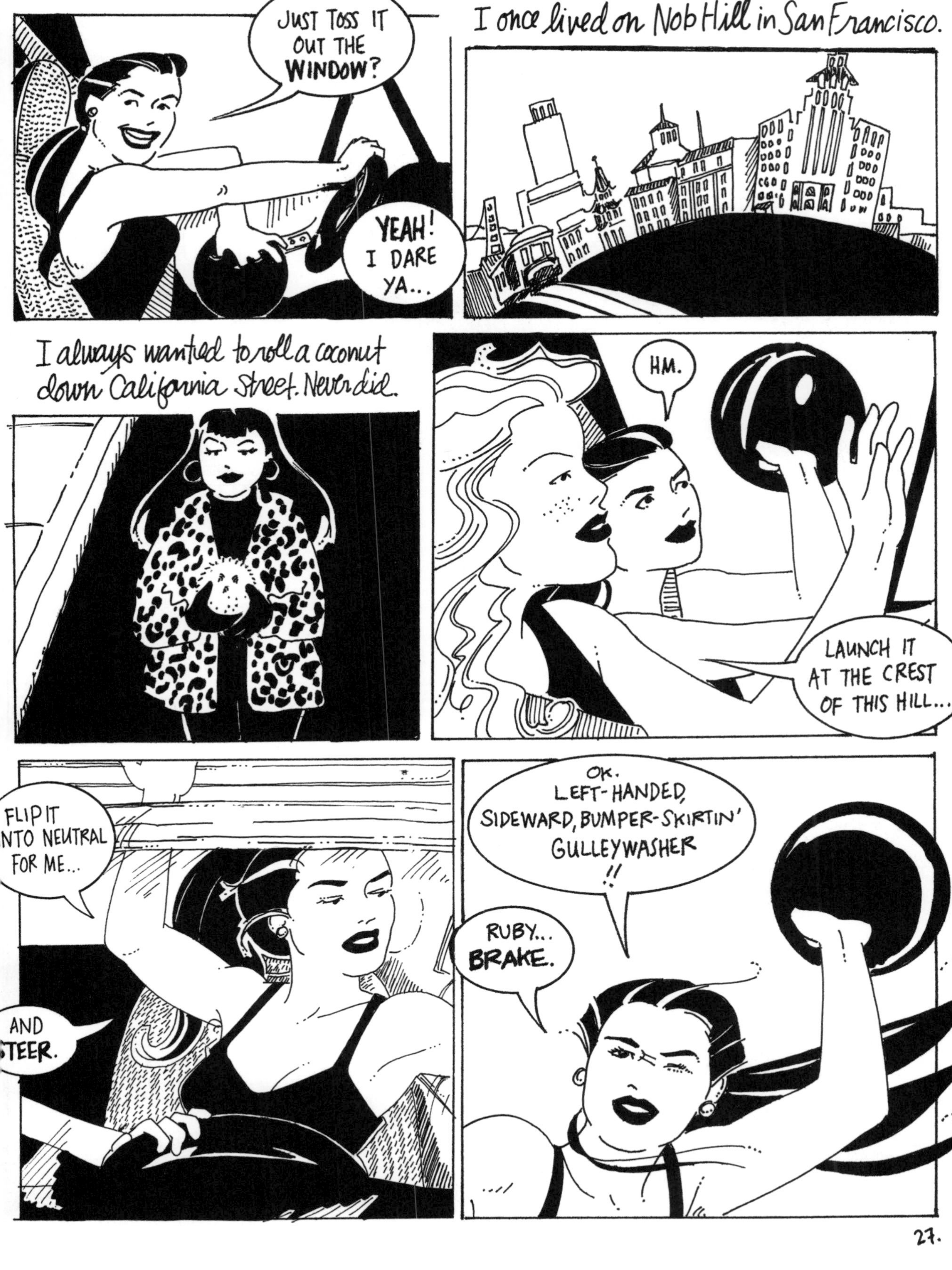
JUST TOSS IT OUT THE WINDOW?
YEAH! I DARE YA...
I once lived on Nob Hill in San Francisco.
I always wanted to roll a coconut down California Street. Never did.
HM.
LAUNCH IT AT THE CREST OF THIS HILL...
FLIP IT NTO NEUTRAL FOR ME...
AND TEER.
OK. LEFT-HANDED, SIDEWARD, BUMPER-SKIRTIN' GULLEYWASHER !!
RUBY... BRAKE.

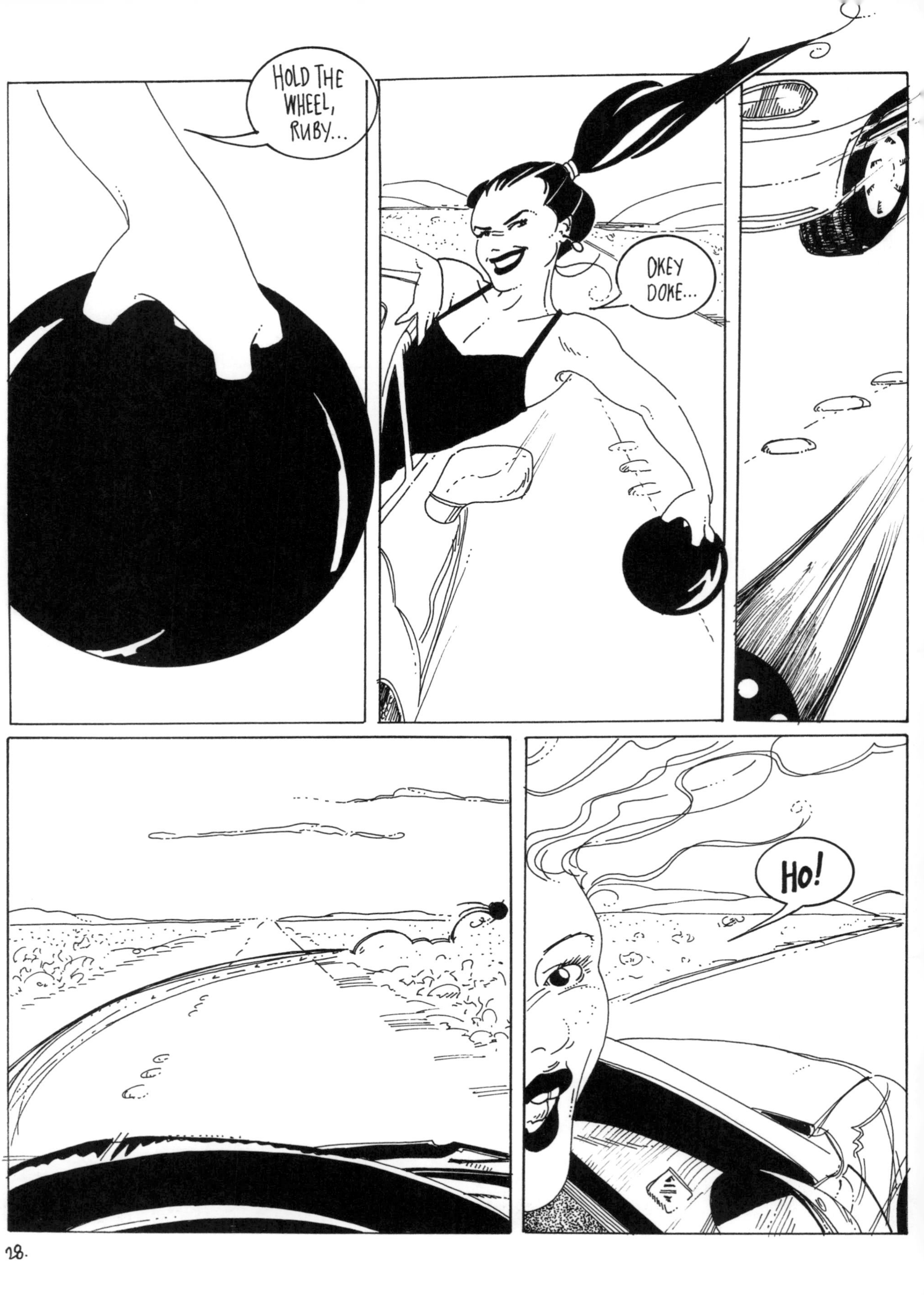
HOLD THE WHEEL, RUBY...
OKEY DOKE...
HO!

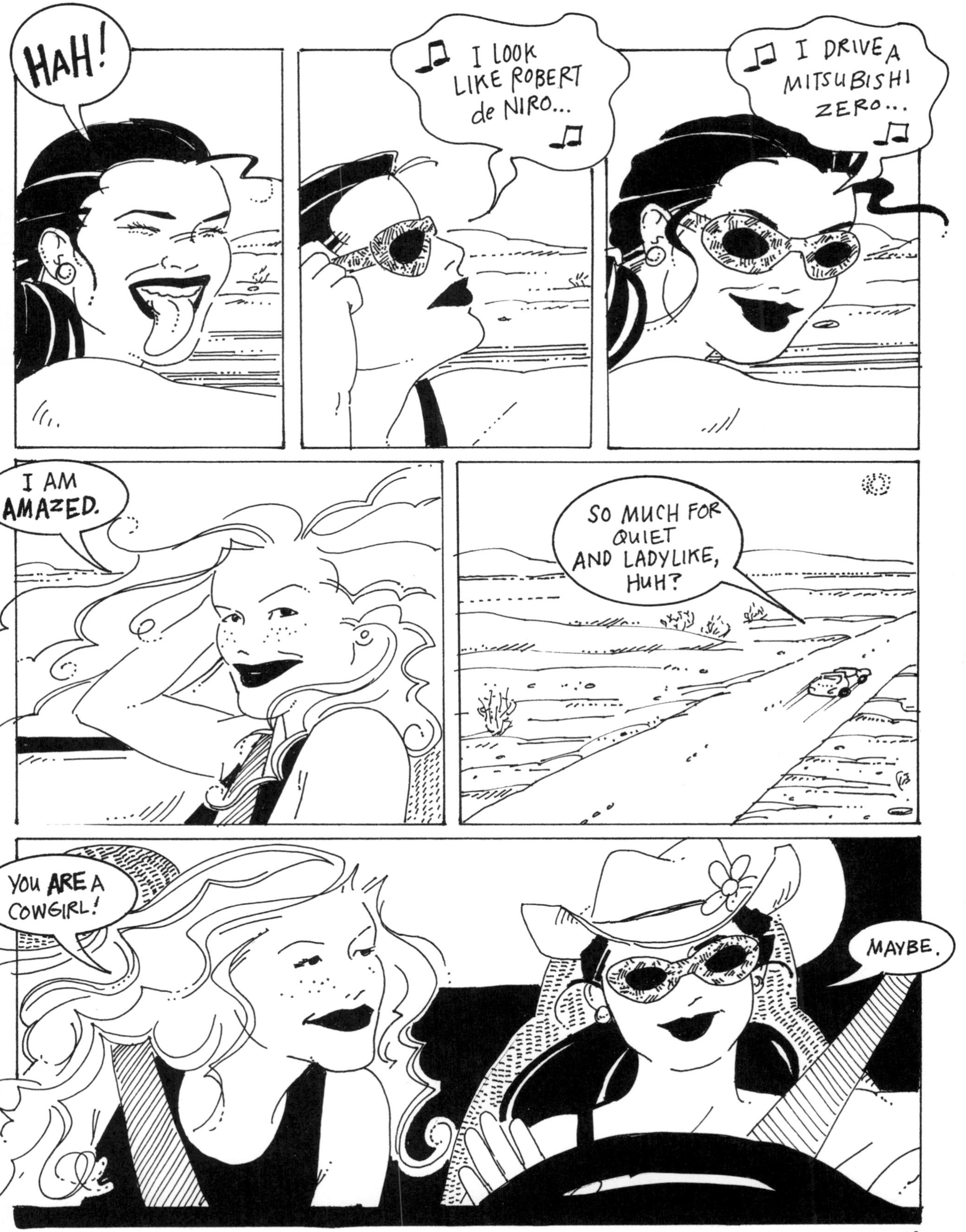

HAH!
I LOOK LIKE ROBERT de NIRO...
I DRIVE A MITSUBISHI ZERO...
I AM AMAZED.
SO MUCH FOR QUIET AND LADYLIKE, HUH?
YOU ARE A COWGIRL!
MAYBE.

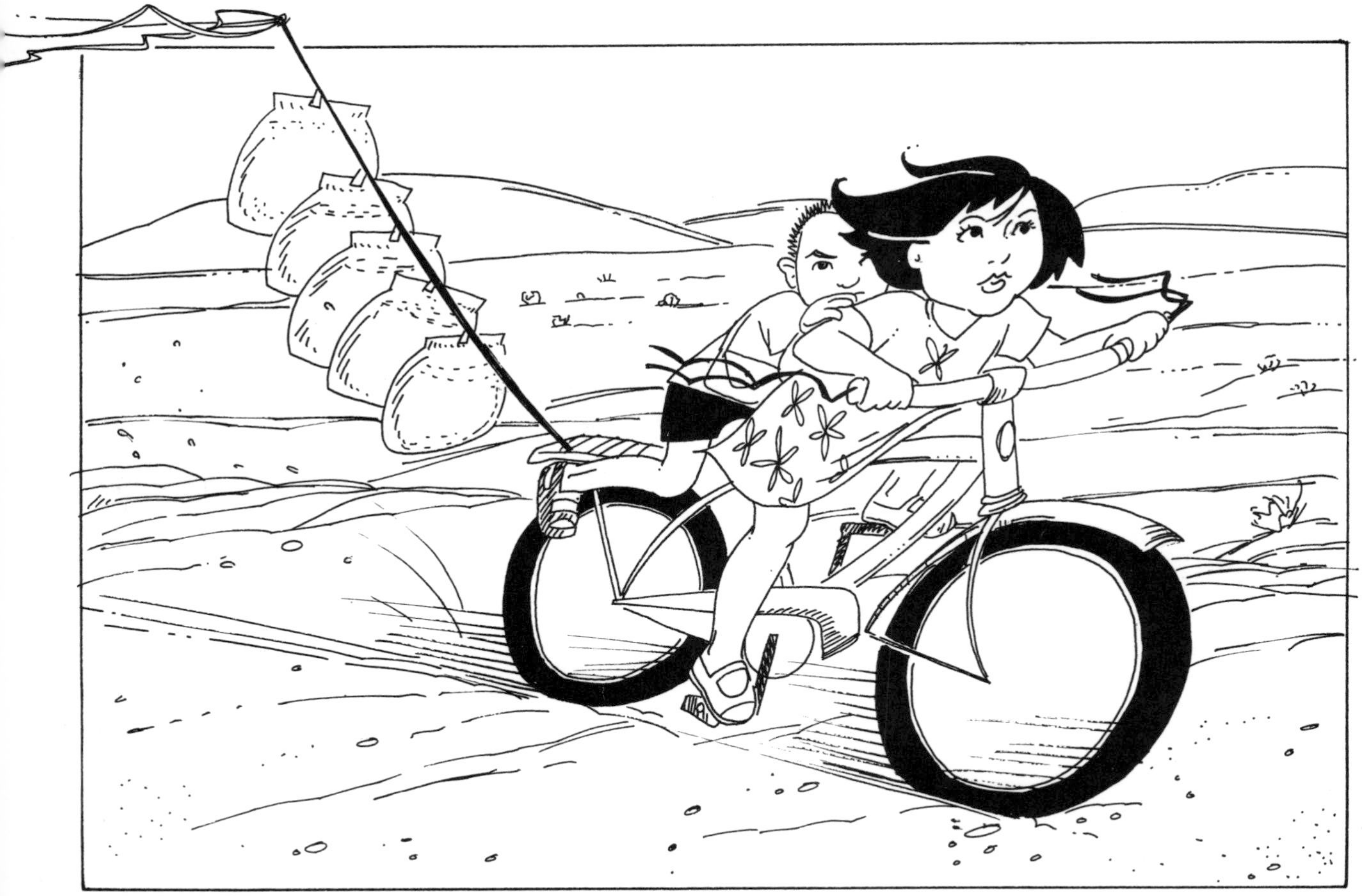

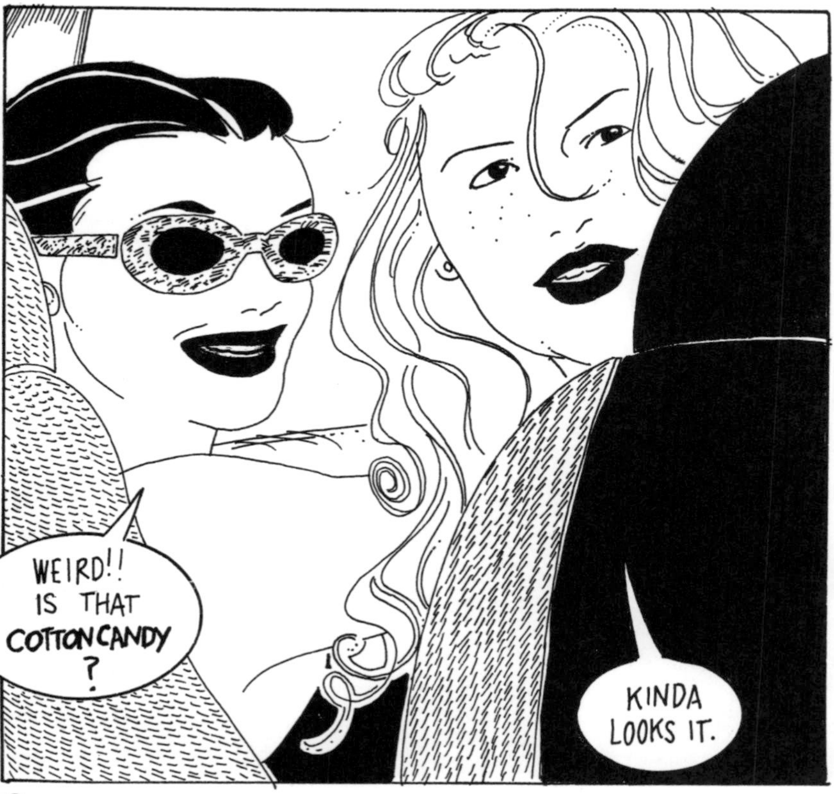
WEIRD!! IS THAT COTTON CANDY ?
KINDA LOOKS IT.

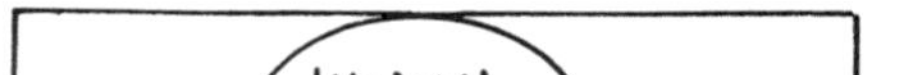
WANNA STOP?
YEAH

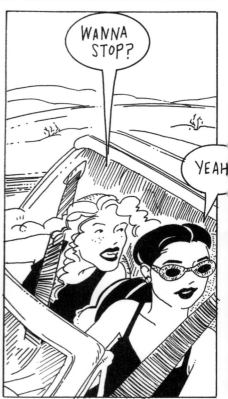

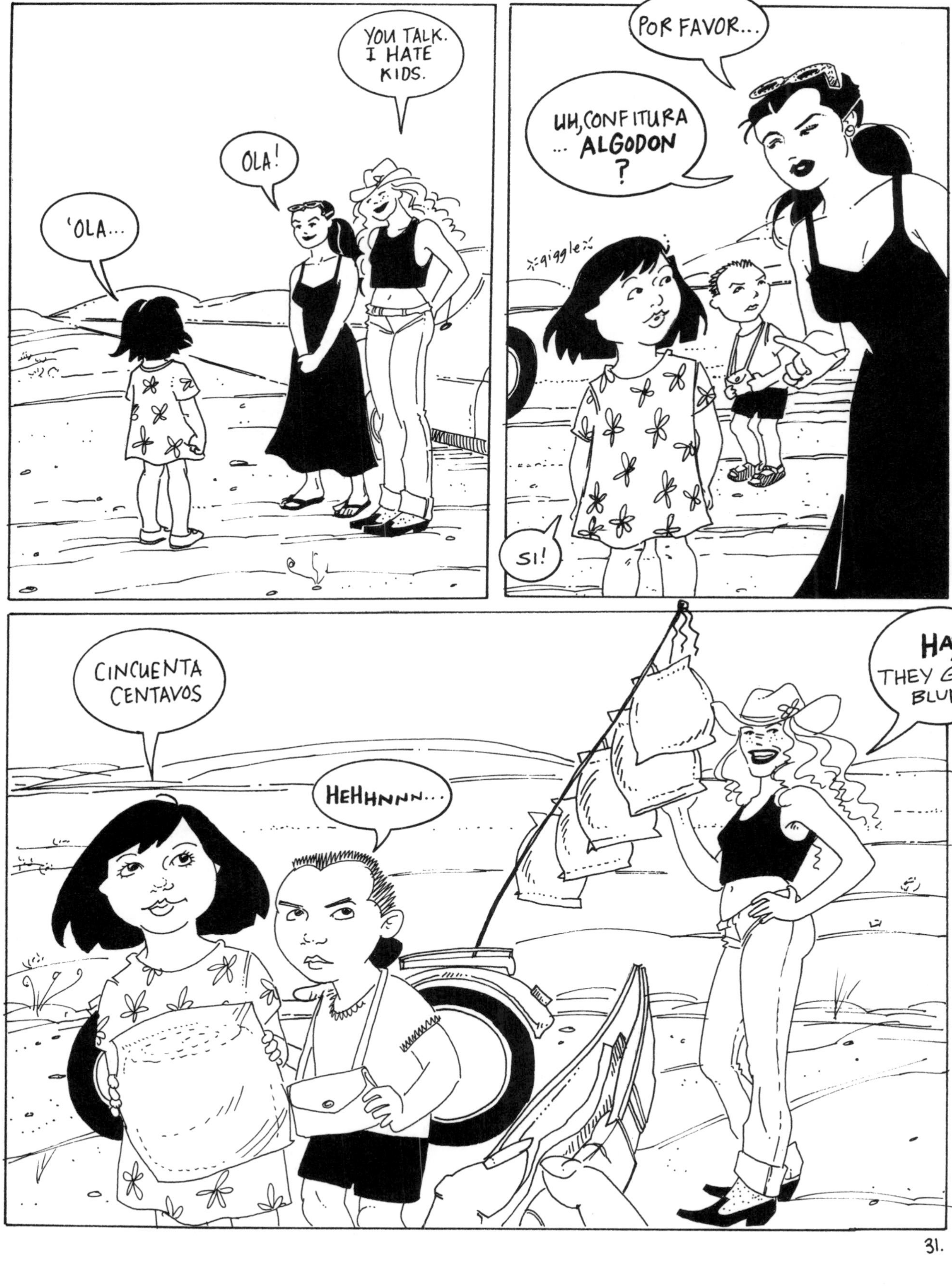
YOU TALK. I HATE KIDS.
OLA!
'OLA...
POR FAVOR...
UH, CONFITURA ... ALGODON ?
giggle
SI!
CINCUENTA CENTAVOS
HEHHNNN...
HAY! THEY GOT BLUE!!

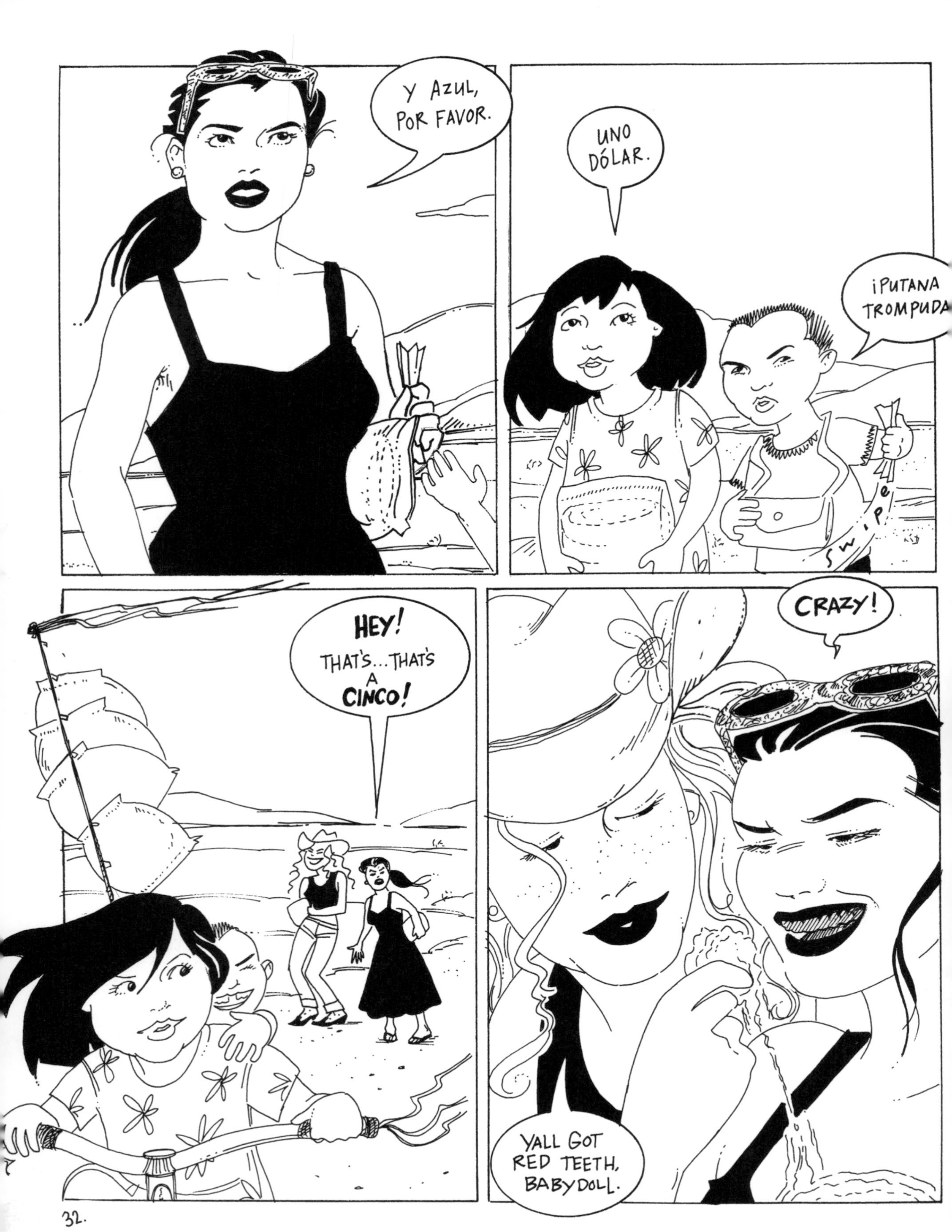
Y AZUL, POR FAVOR.
UNO DÓLAR.
¡PUTANA TROMPUDA
SWIPE
HEY! THAT'S... THAT'S A CINCO!
CRAZY!
YALL GOT RED TEETH, BABYDOLL.

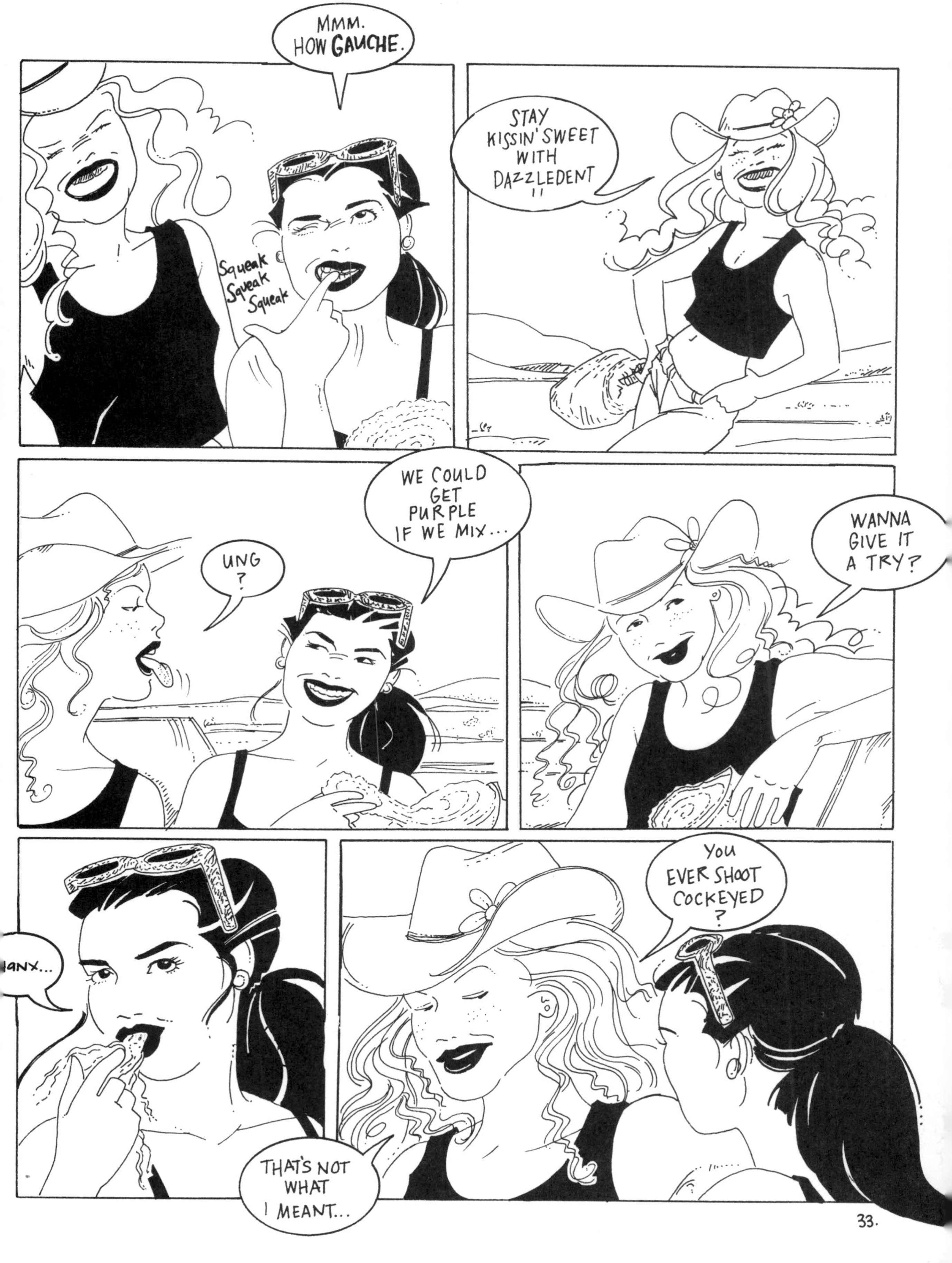
MMM. HOW GAUCHE.
Squeak Squeak Squeak
STAY KISSIN' SWEET WITH DAZZLEDENT
UNG ?
WE COULD GET PURPLE IF WE MIX...
WANNA GIVE IT A TRY?
HANX...
YOU EVER SHOOT COCKEYED ?
THAT'S NOT WHAT I MEANT...
.....

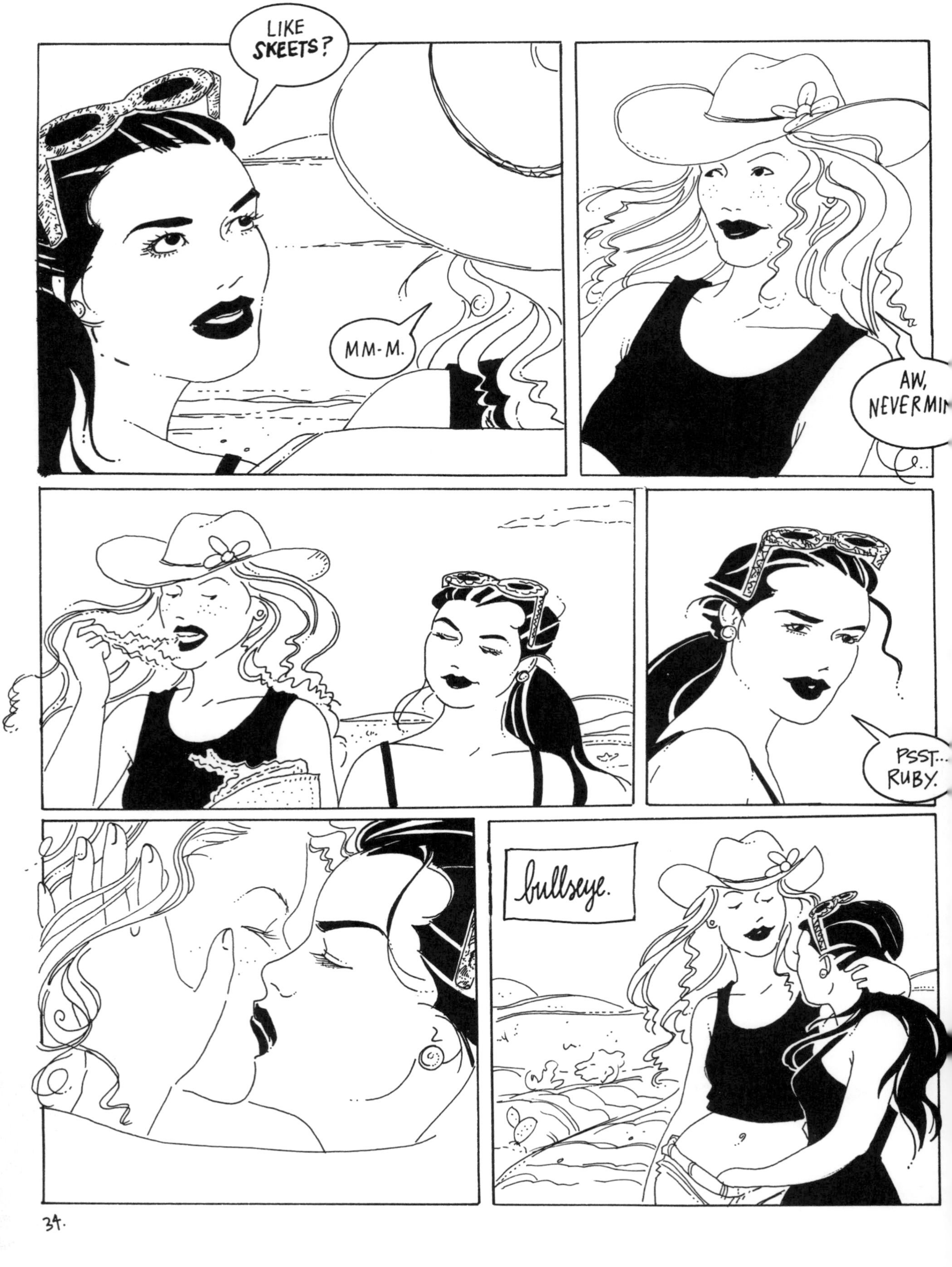
LIKE SKEETS?
MM-M.
AW, NEVERMIN
PSST... RUBY.
bullseye.

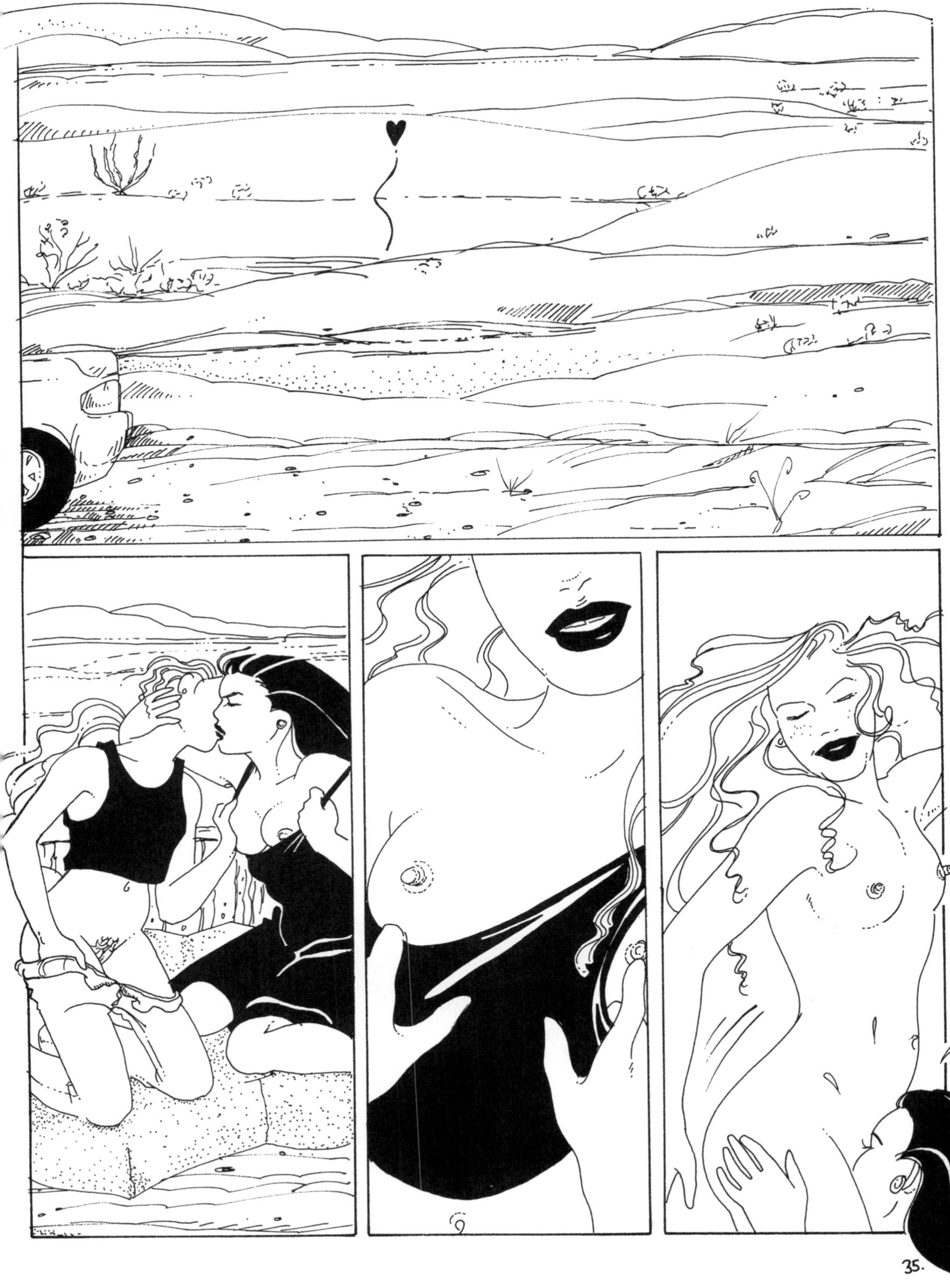

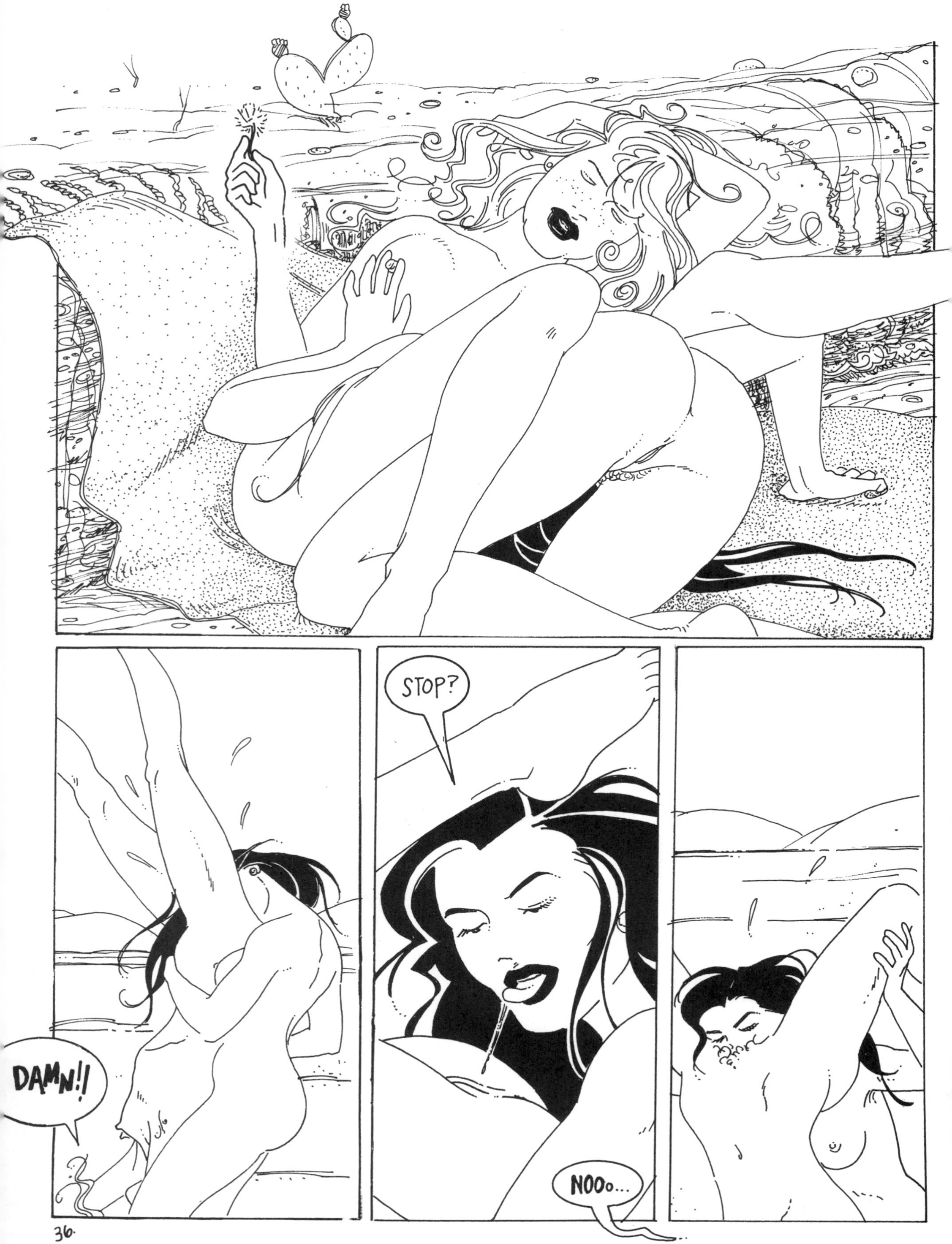
DAMN!!
STOP?
NOOo...

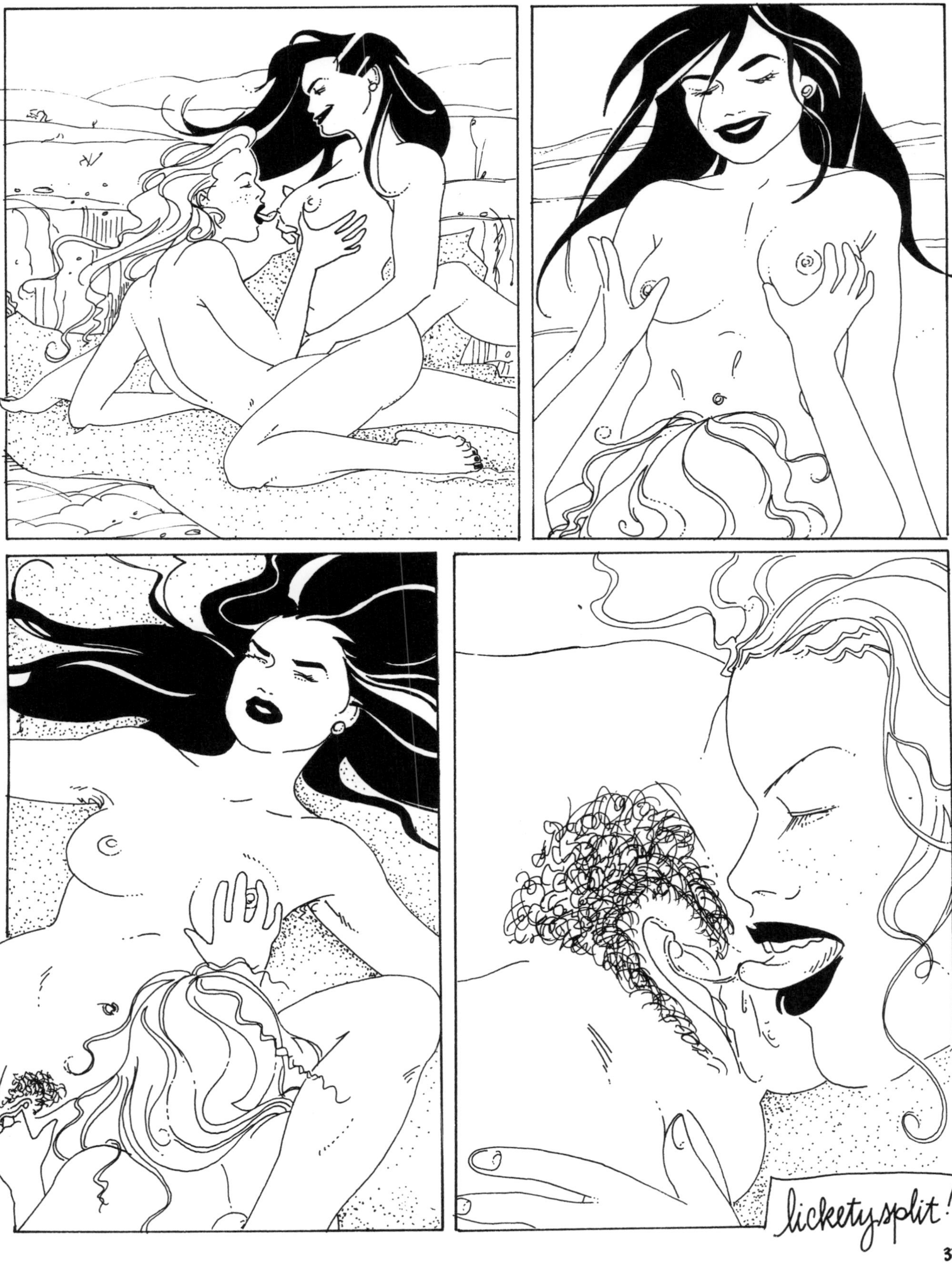
licketysplit!

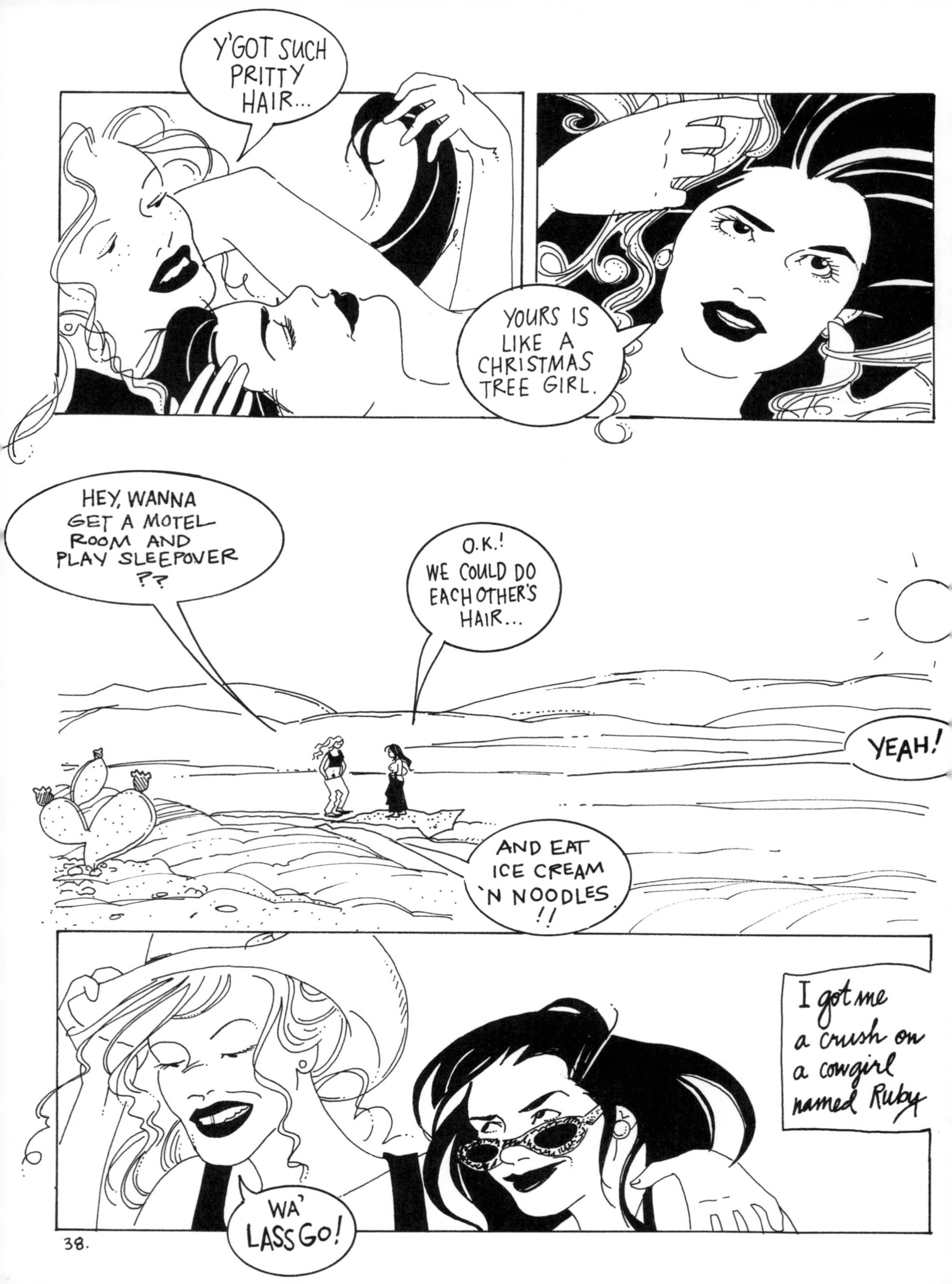
Y'GOT SUCH PRITTY HAIR...
YOURS IS LIKE A CHRISTMAS TREE GIRL.
HEY, WANNA GET A MOTEL ROOM AND PLAY SLEEPOVER ??
O.K.! WE COULD DO EACH OTHER'S HAIR...
YEAH!
AND EAT ICE CREAM 'N NOODLES !!
I got me a crush on a cowgirl named Ruby
WA' LASS GO!

At the Ⓚ

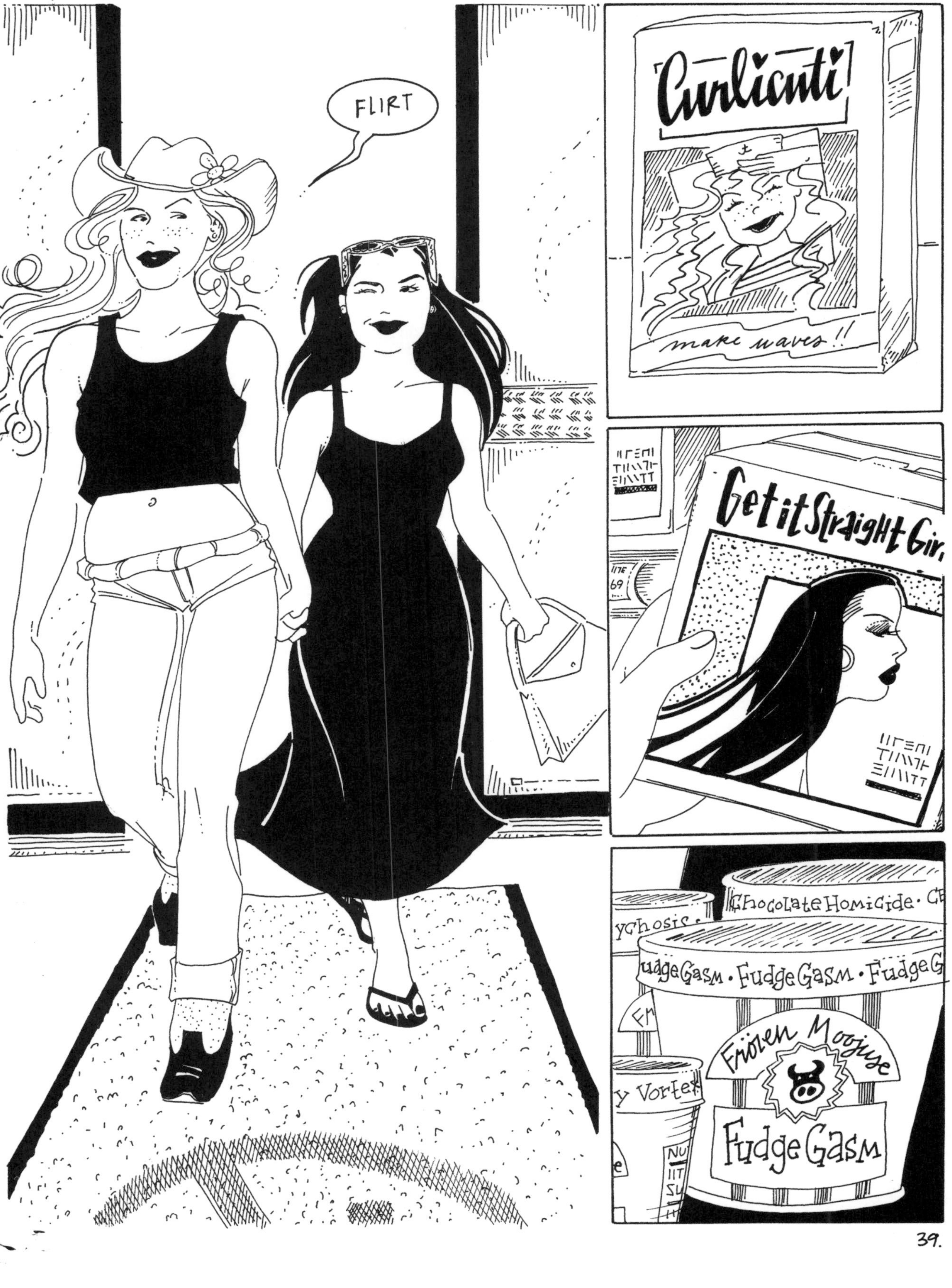

FLIRT
Curlicuti
make waves!!
Get it Straight Gir
Chocolate Homicide
FudgeGasm · FudgeGasm · FudgeG
Frözen Moojuse
FudgeGasm
y Vortex

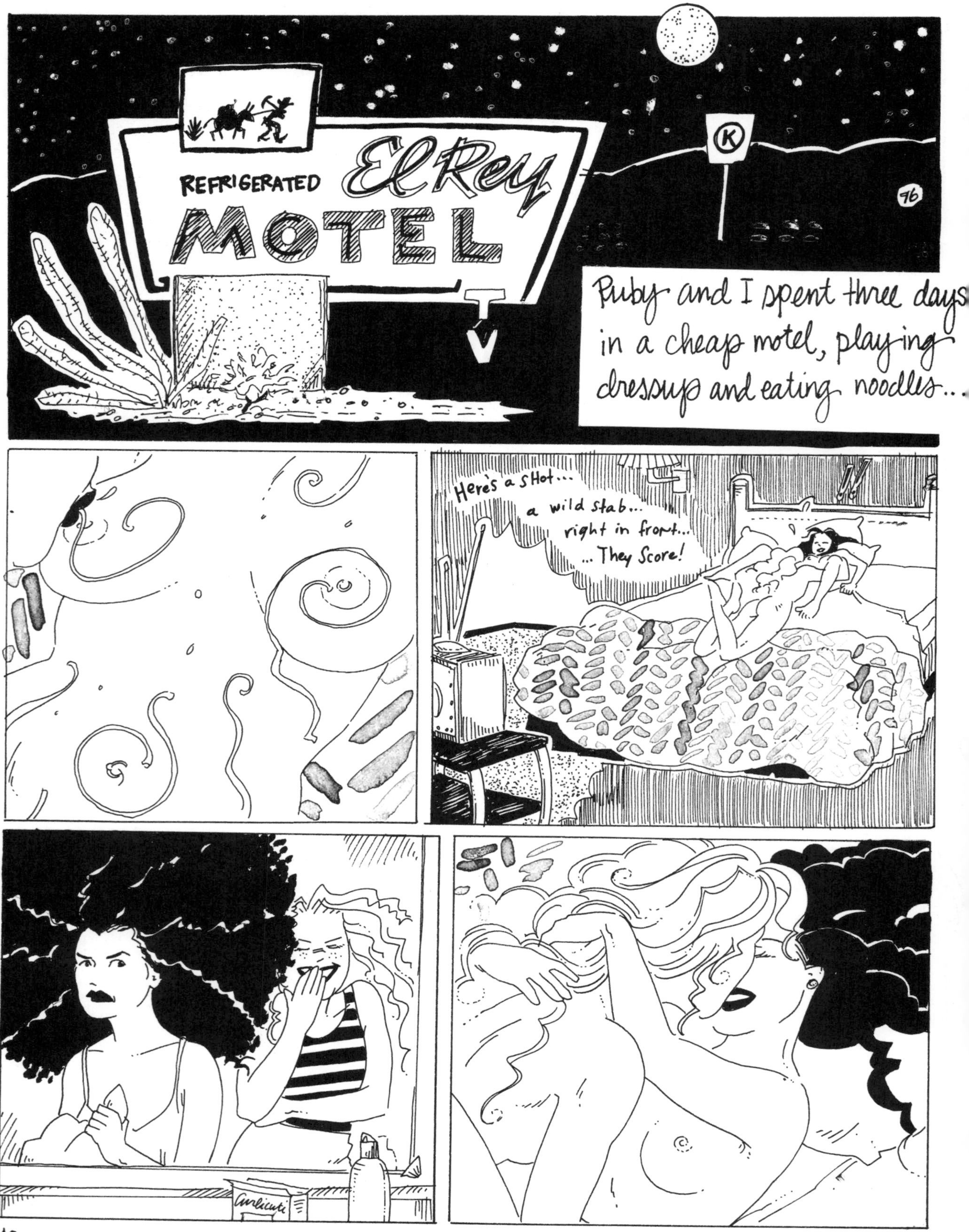
El Rey
REFRIGERATED
MOTEL
TV
K
76
Ruby and I spent three days in a cheap motel, playing dressup and eating noodles...
Here's a sHot...
a wild stab...
right in front...
...They Score!

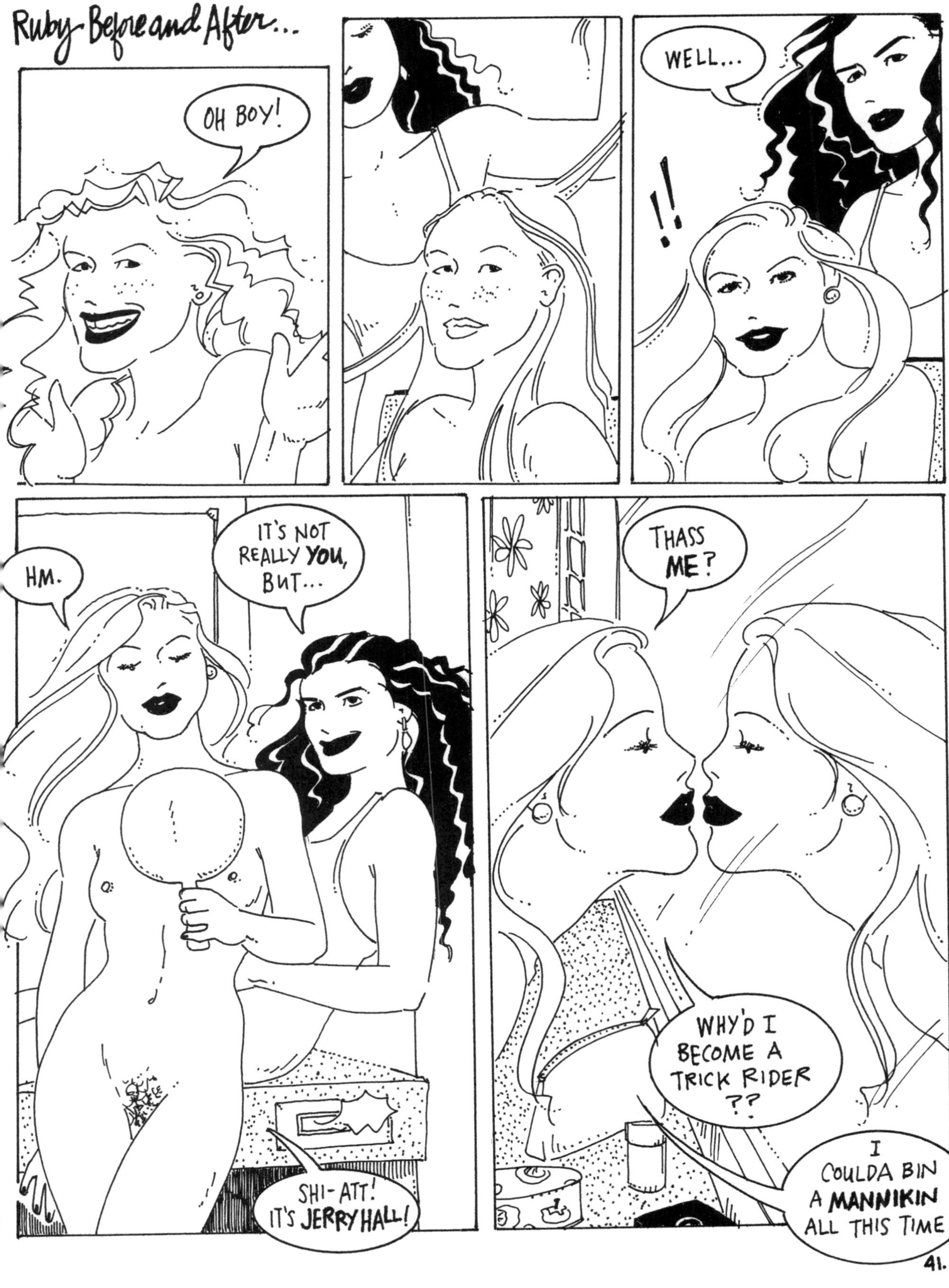
Ruby-Before and After...
OH BOY!
WELL...
!!
HM.
IT'S NOT REALLY YOU, BUT...
SHI-ATT! IT'S JERRY HALL!
THASS ME?
WHY'D I BECOME A TRICK RIDER ??
I COULDA BIN A MANNIKIN ALL THIS TIME!

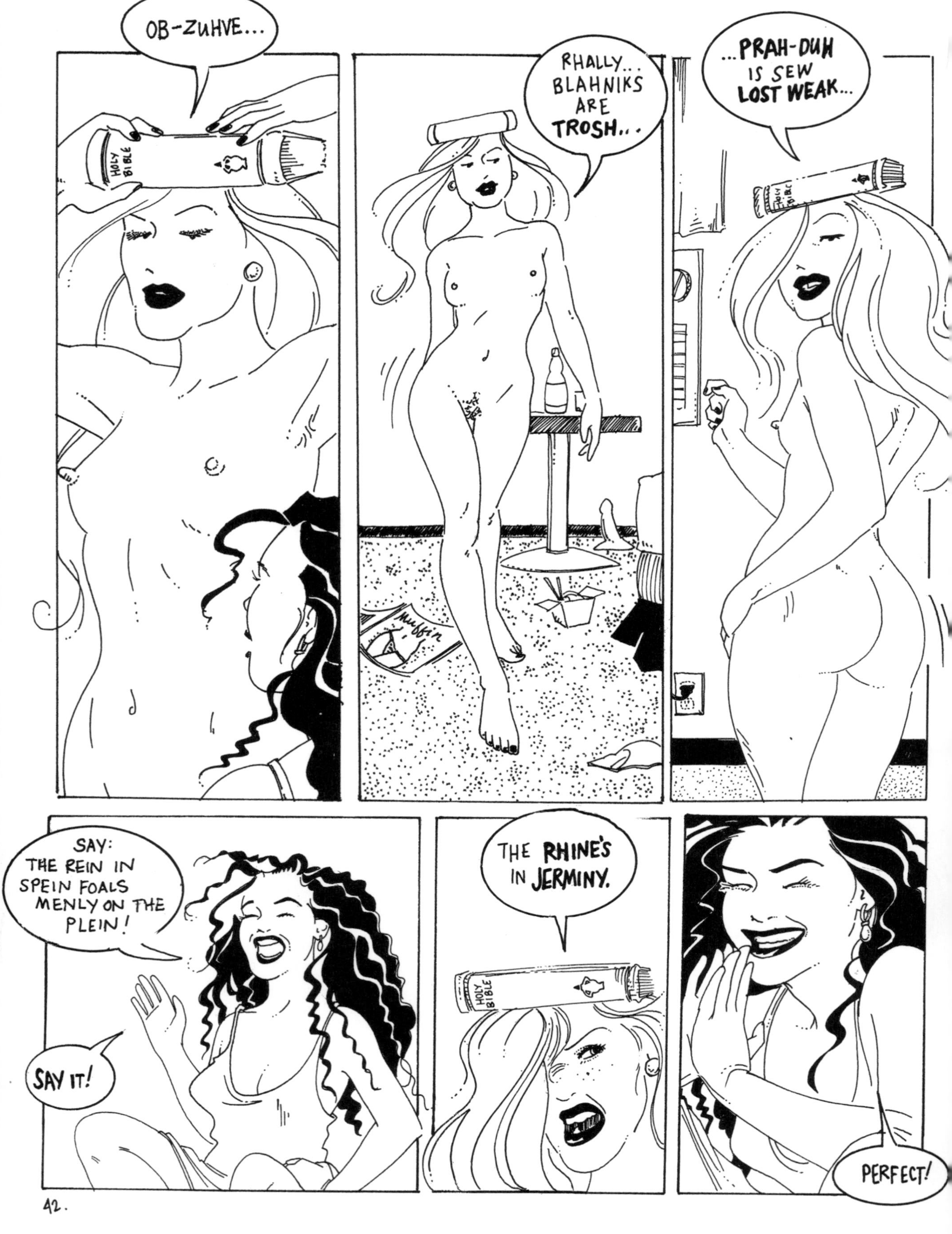
OB-ZUHVE...
HOLY BIBLE
RHALLY... BLAHNIKS ARE TROSH...
Muffin
...PRAH-DUH IS SEW LOST WEAK...
HOLY BIBLE
SAY: THE REIN IN SPEIN FOALS MENLY ON THE PLEIN!
SAY IT!
THE RHINE'S IN JERMINY.
HOLY BIBLE
PERFECT!

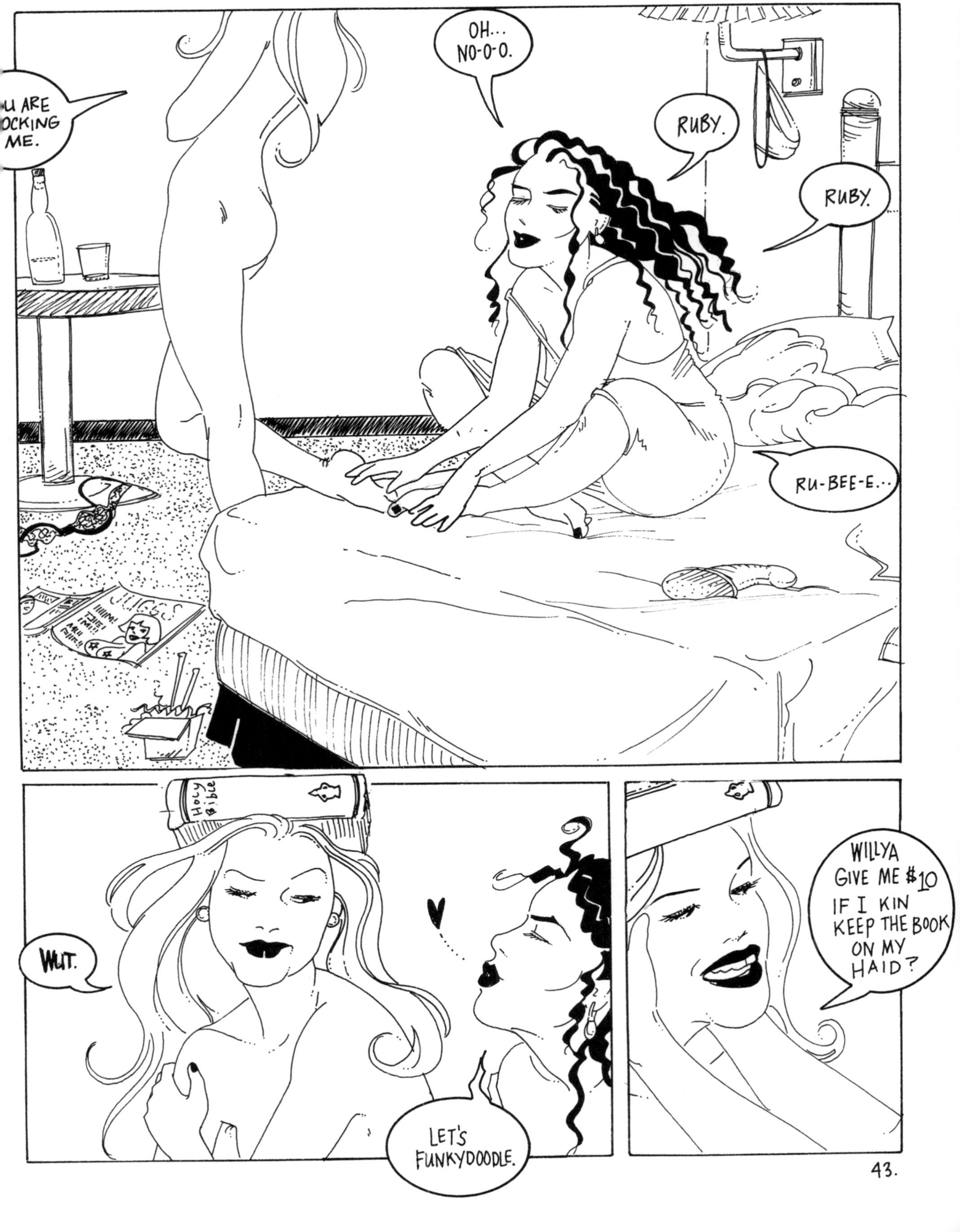
U ARE OCKING ME.
OH... NO-O-O.
RUBY.
RUBY.
RU-BEE-E...
Holy Bible
WUT.
LET'S FUNKYDOODLE.
WILLYA GIVE ME $10 IF I KIN KEEP THE BOOK ON MY HAID?

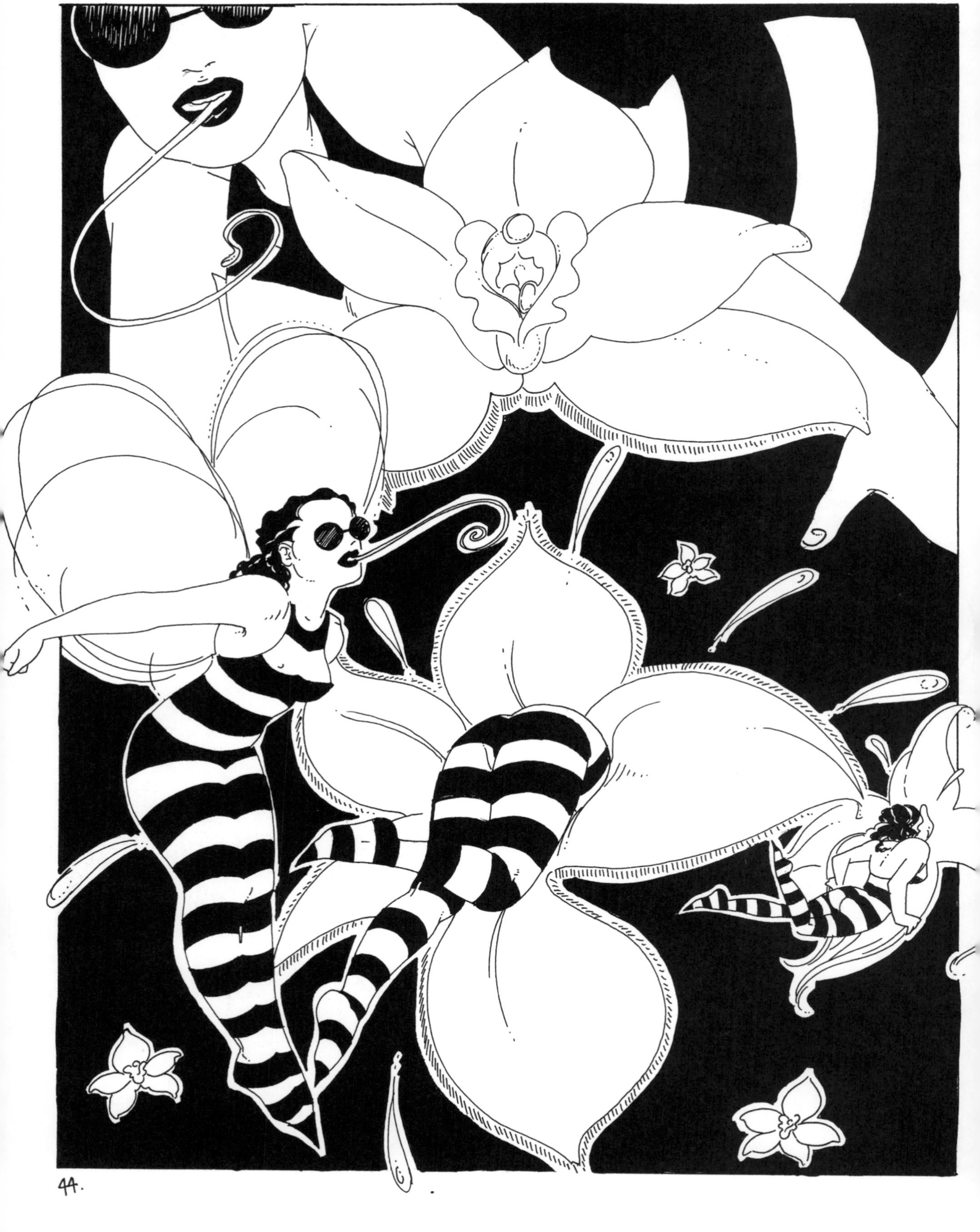

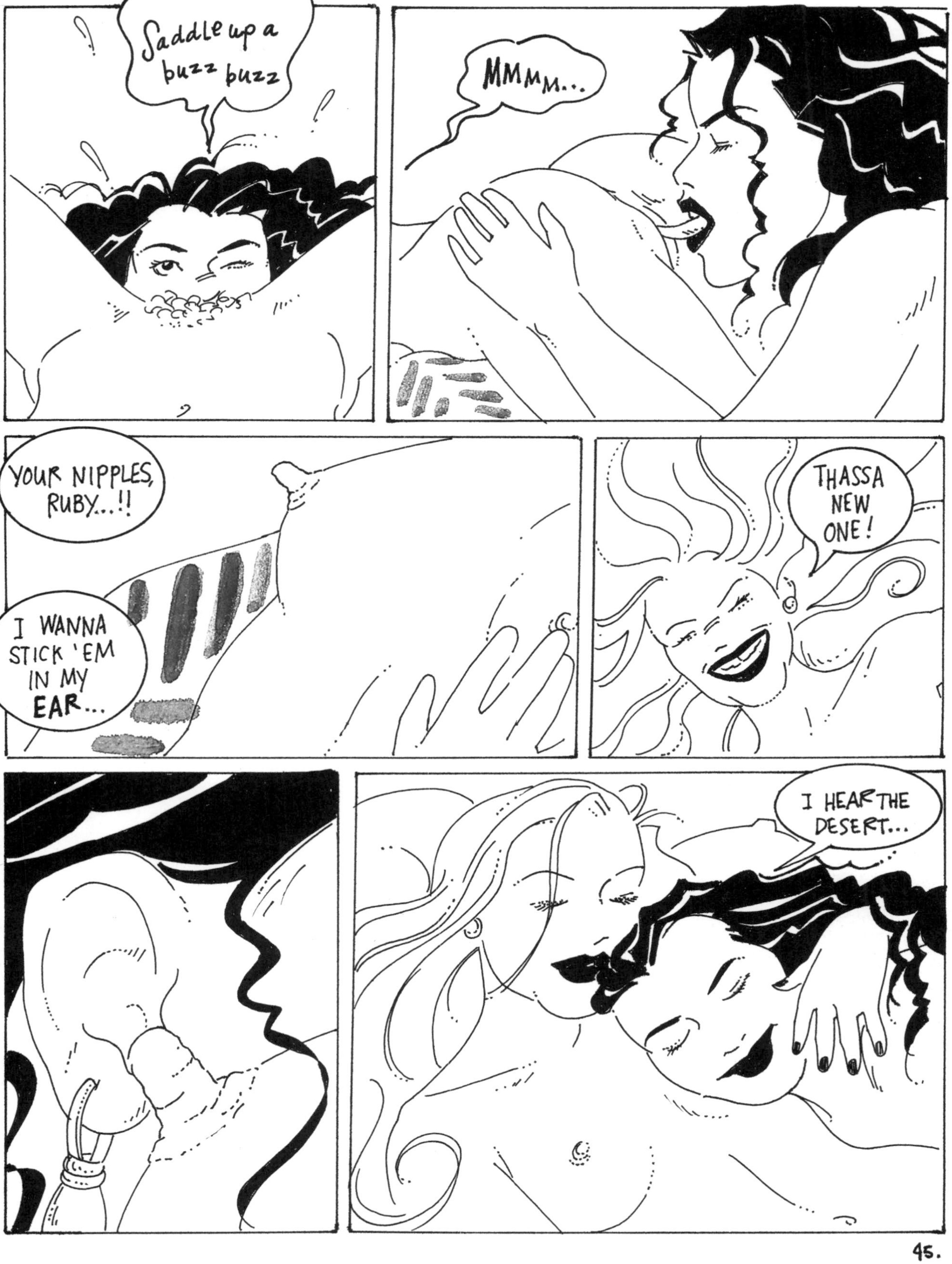
Saddle up a buzz buzz
MMMM...
YOUR NIPPLES, RUBY...!!
I WANNA STICK 'EM IN MY EAR...
THASSA NEW ONE!
I HEAR THE DESERT...

The last night...

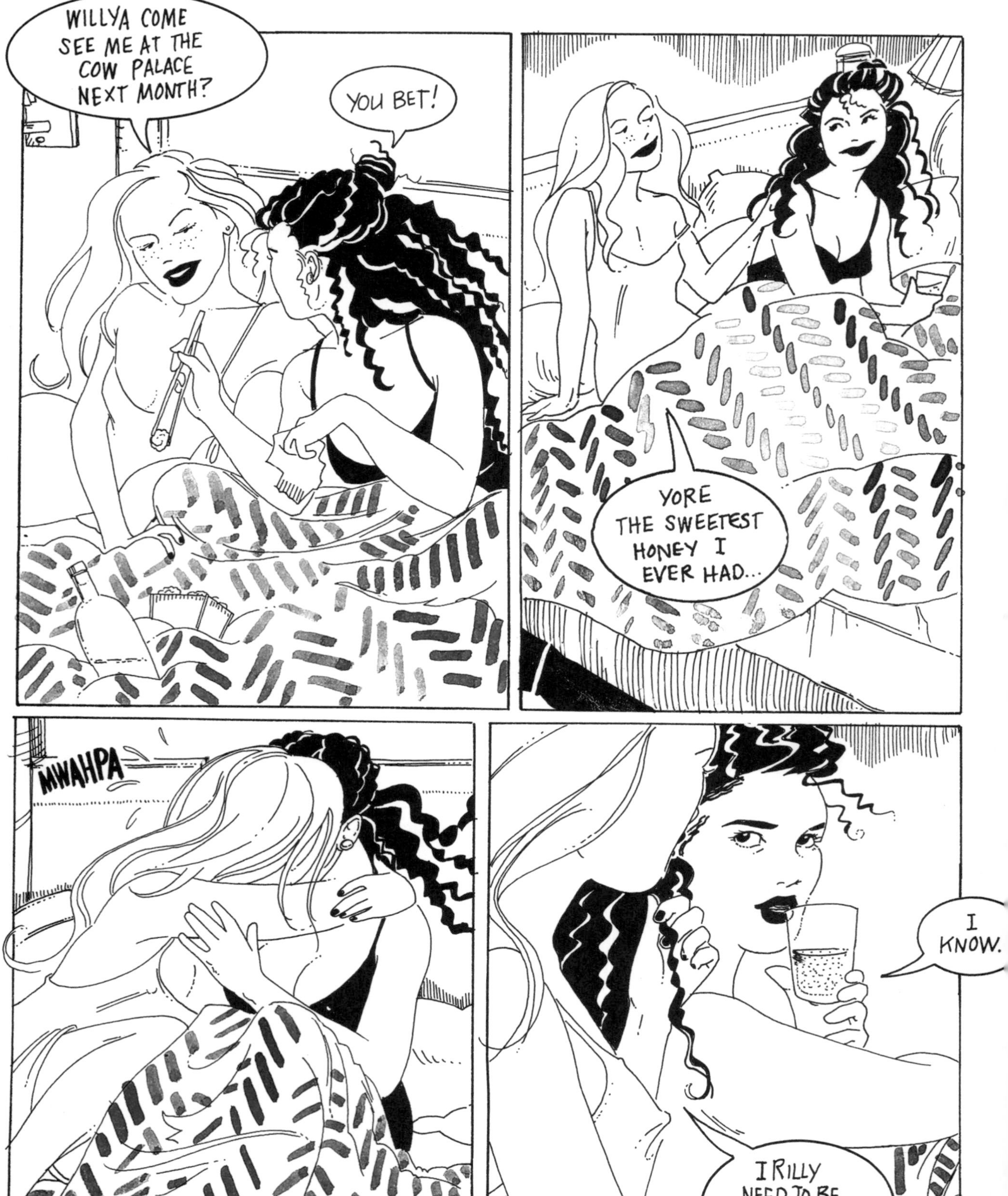

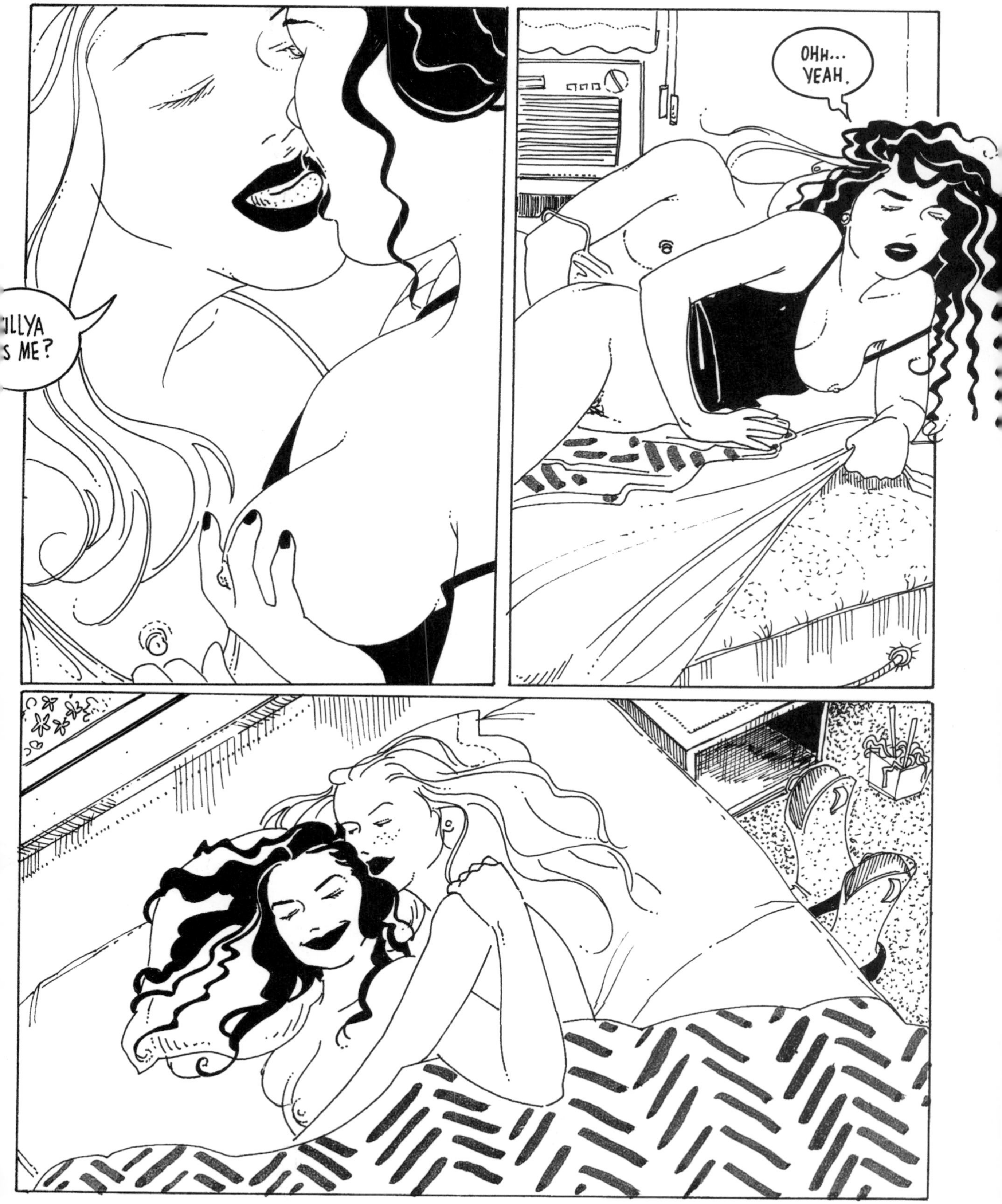
ILLYA
S ME?
OHH... YEAH.

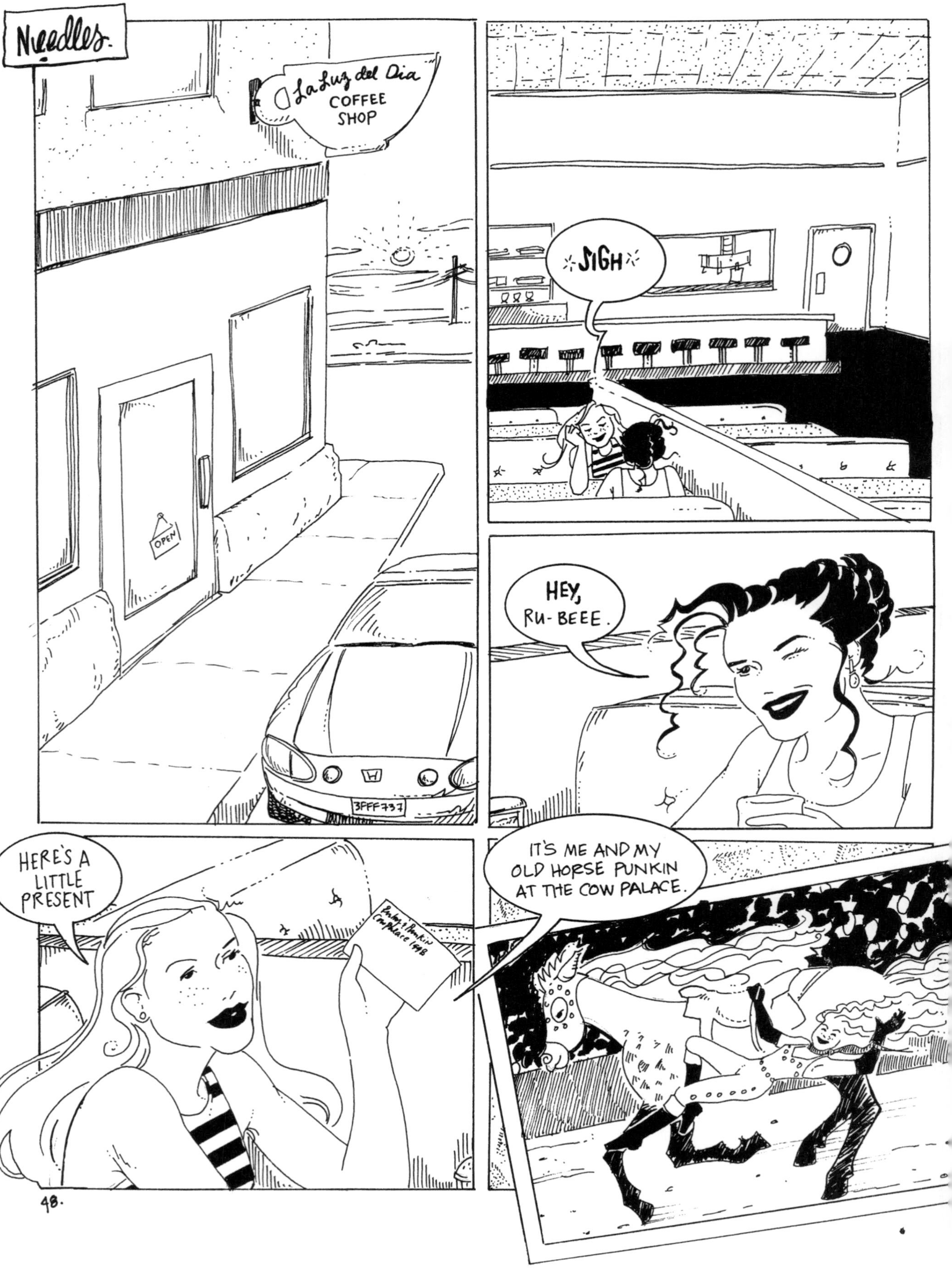
Needles.
La Luz del Dia COFFEE SHOP
OPEN
3FFF737
SIGH
HEY, RU-BEEE.
HERE'S A LITTLE PRESENT
IT'S ME AND MY OLD HORSE PUNKIN AT THE COW PALACE.

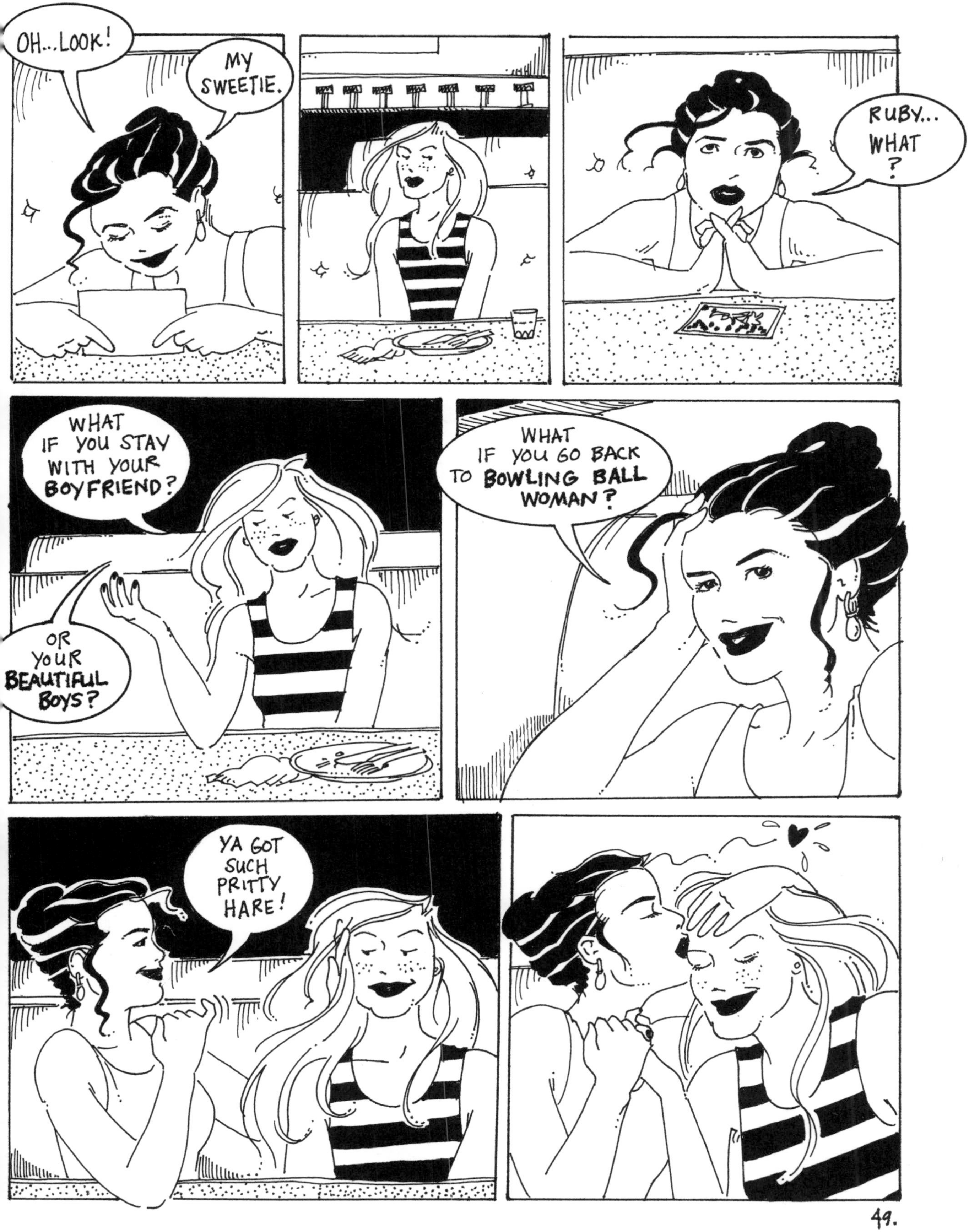
OH...LOOK!
MY SWEETIE.
RUBY... WHAT ?
WHAT IF YOU STAY WITH YOUR BOYFRIEND?
OR YOUR BEAUTIFUL BOYS?
WHAT IF YOU GO BACK TO BOWLING BALL WOMAN?
YA GOT SUCH PRITTY HARE!

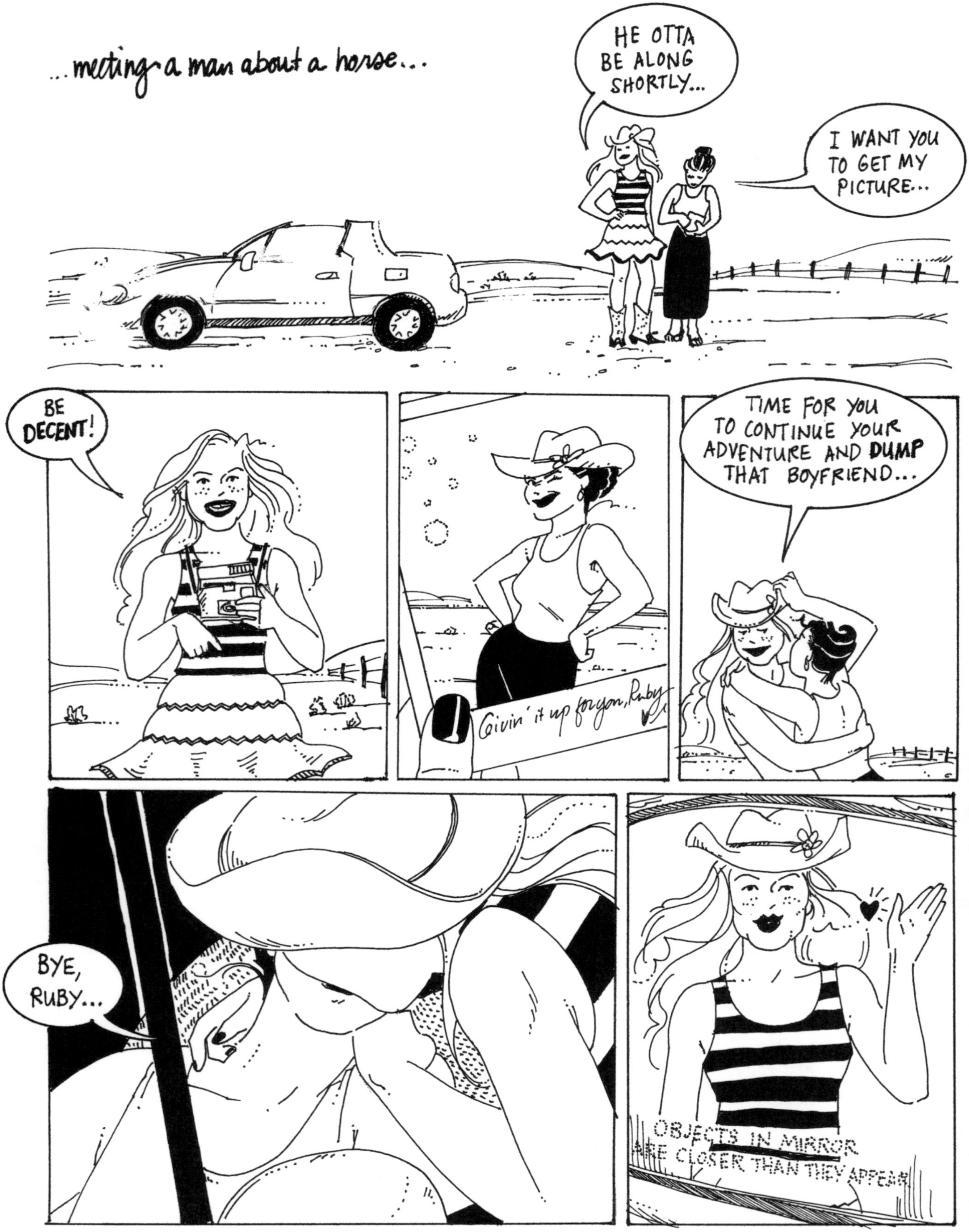
...meeting a man about a horse...
HE OTTA BE ALONG SHORTLY...
I WANT YOU TO GET MY PICTURE...
BE DECENT!
Givin' it up for you, Ruby
TIME FOR YOU TO CONTINUE YOUR ADVENTURE AND DUMP THAT BOYFRIEND...
BYE, RUBY...
OBJECTS IN MIRROR ARE CLOSER THAN THEY APPEAR

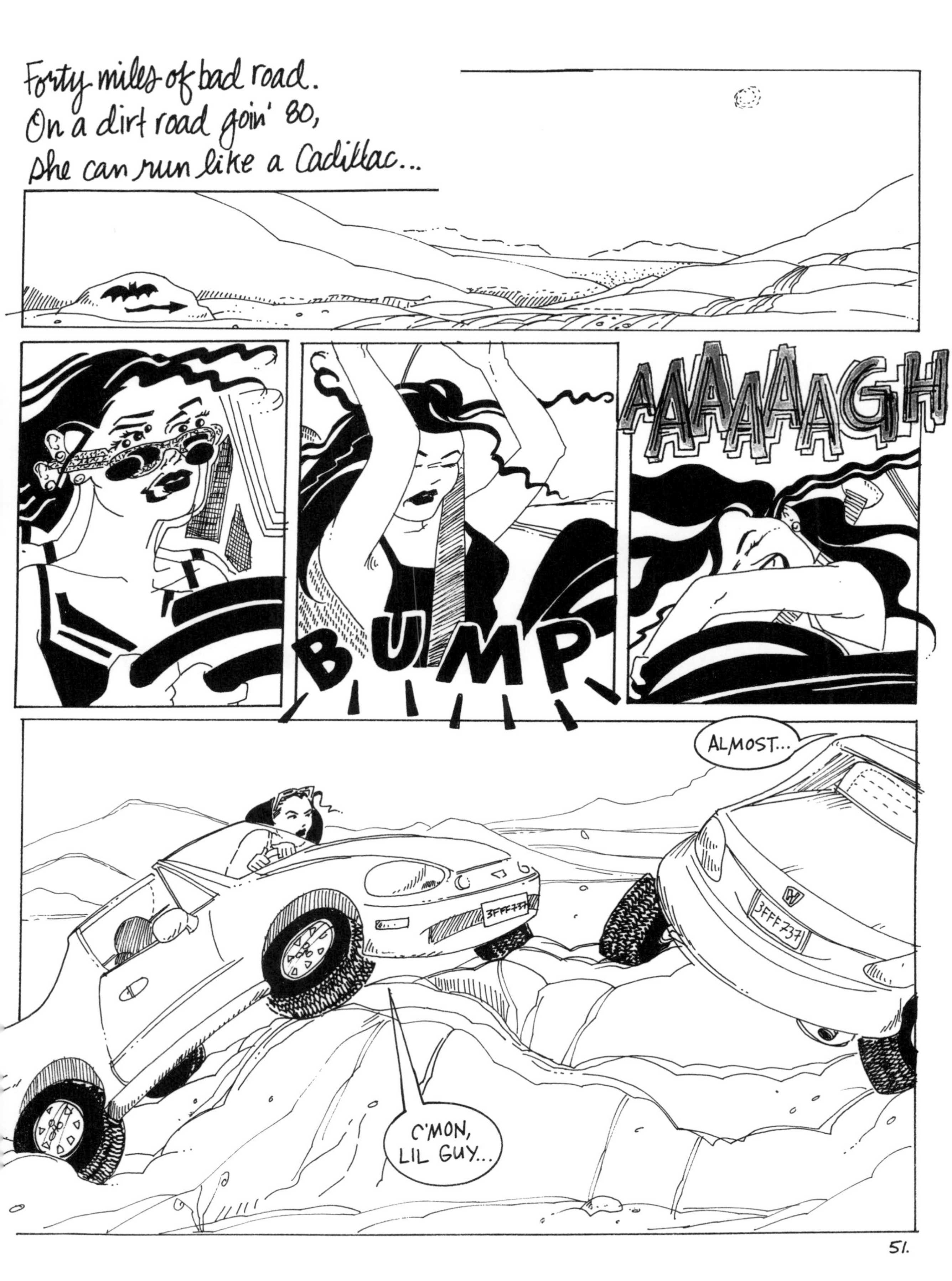
Forty miles of bad road.
On a dirt road goin' 80,
she can run like a Cadillac...
BUMP
AAAAAAGH
ALMOST...
C'MON, LIL GUY...

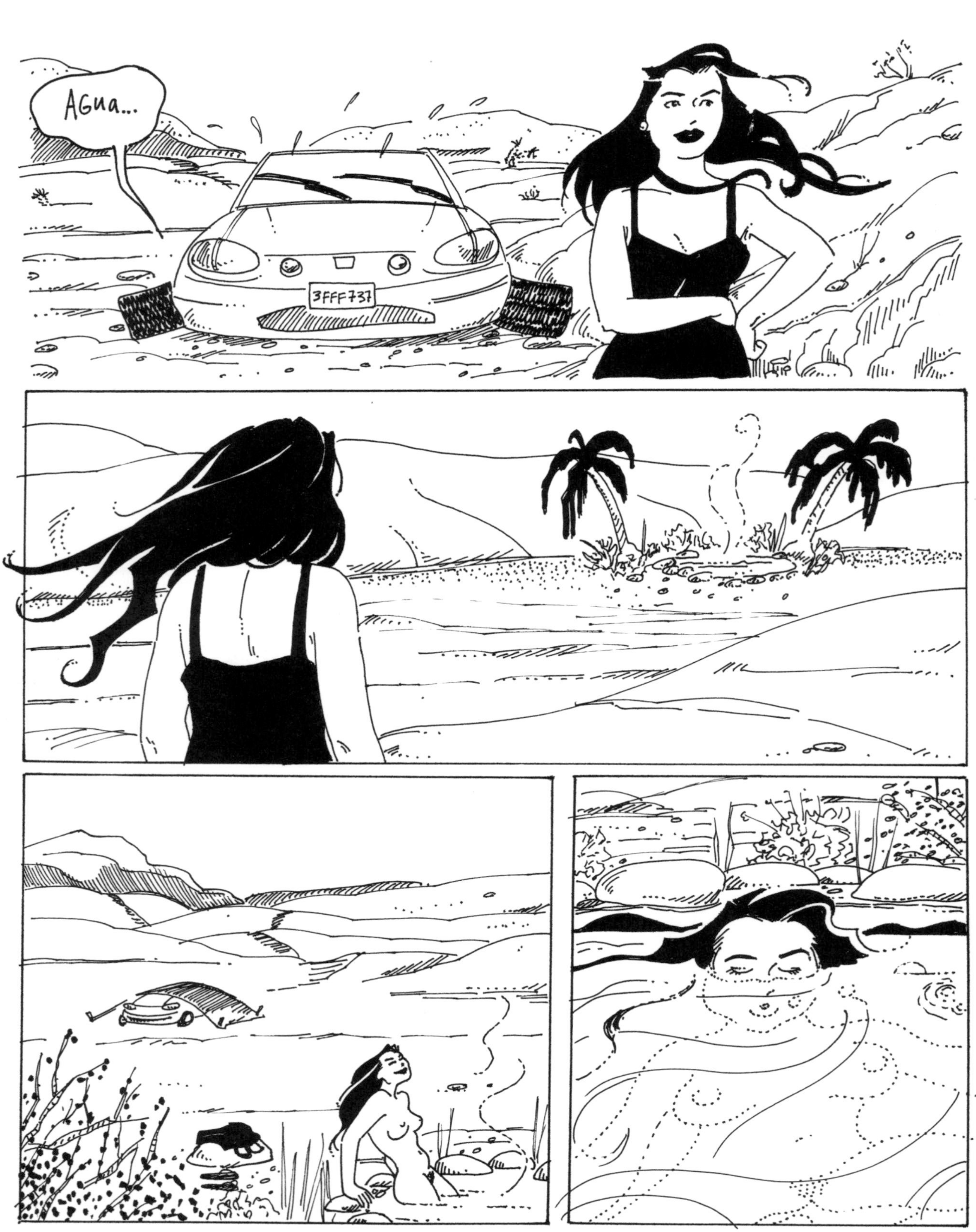
Agua...
3FFF737

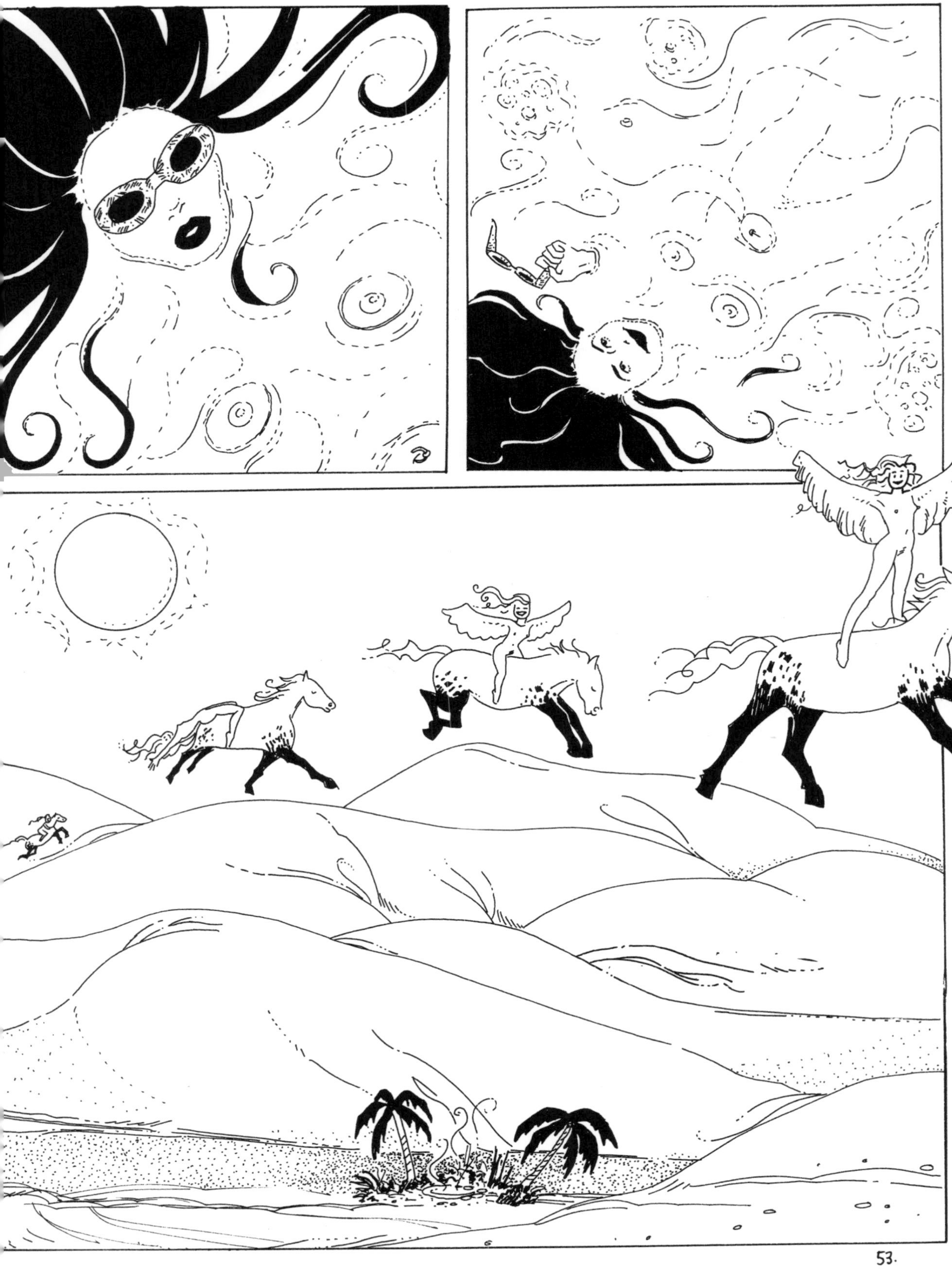

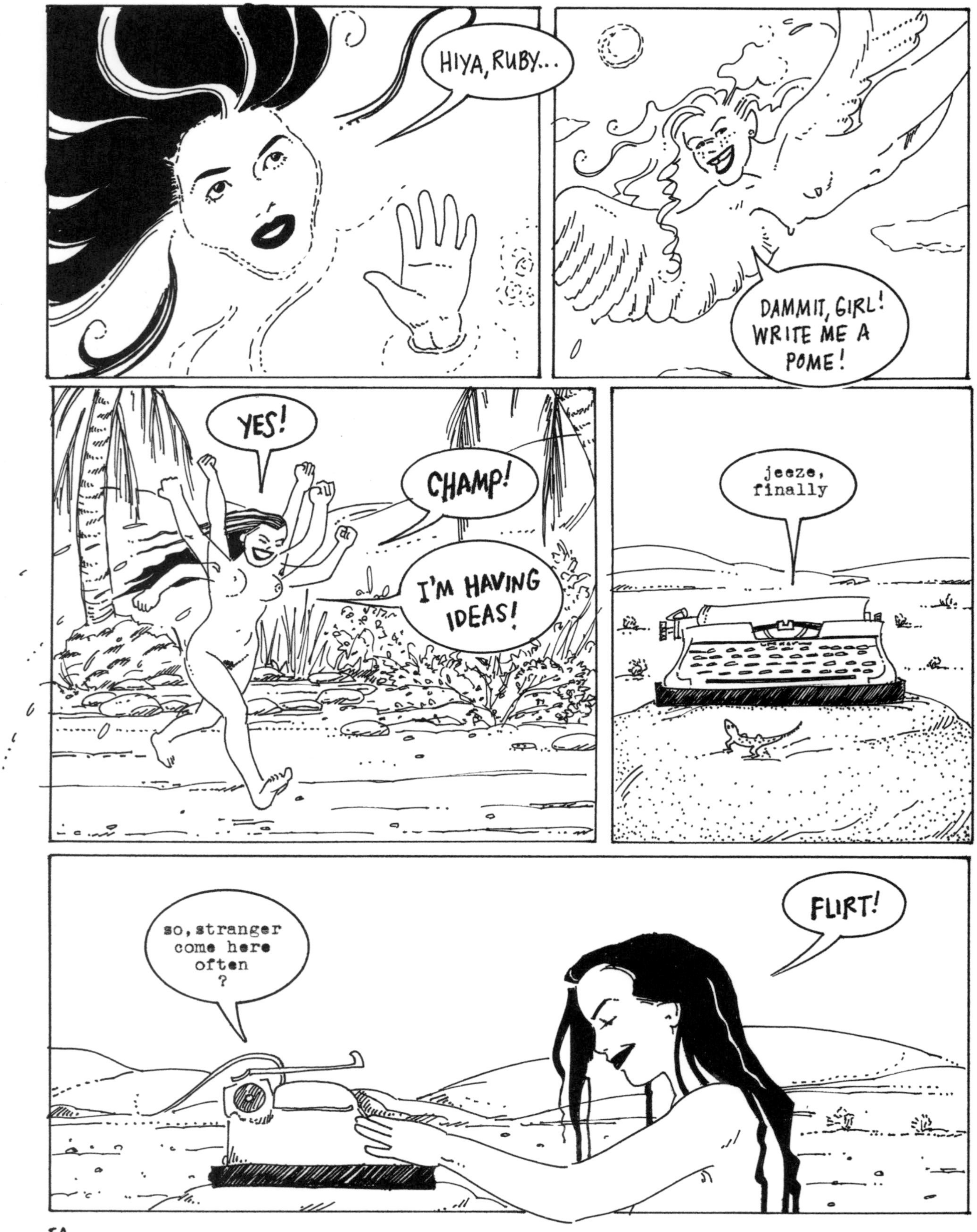
HIYA, RUBY...
DAMMIT, GIRL! WRITE ME A POME!
YES!
CHAMP!
I'M HAVING IDEAS!
jeeze, finally
so, stranger come here often ?
FLIRT!

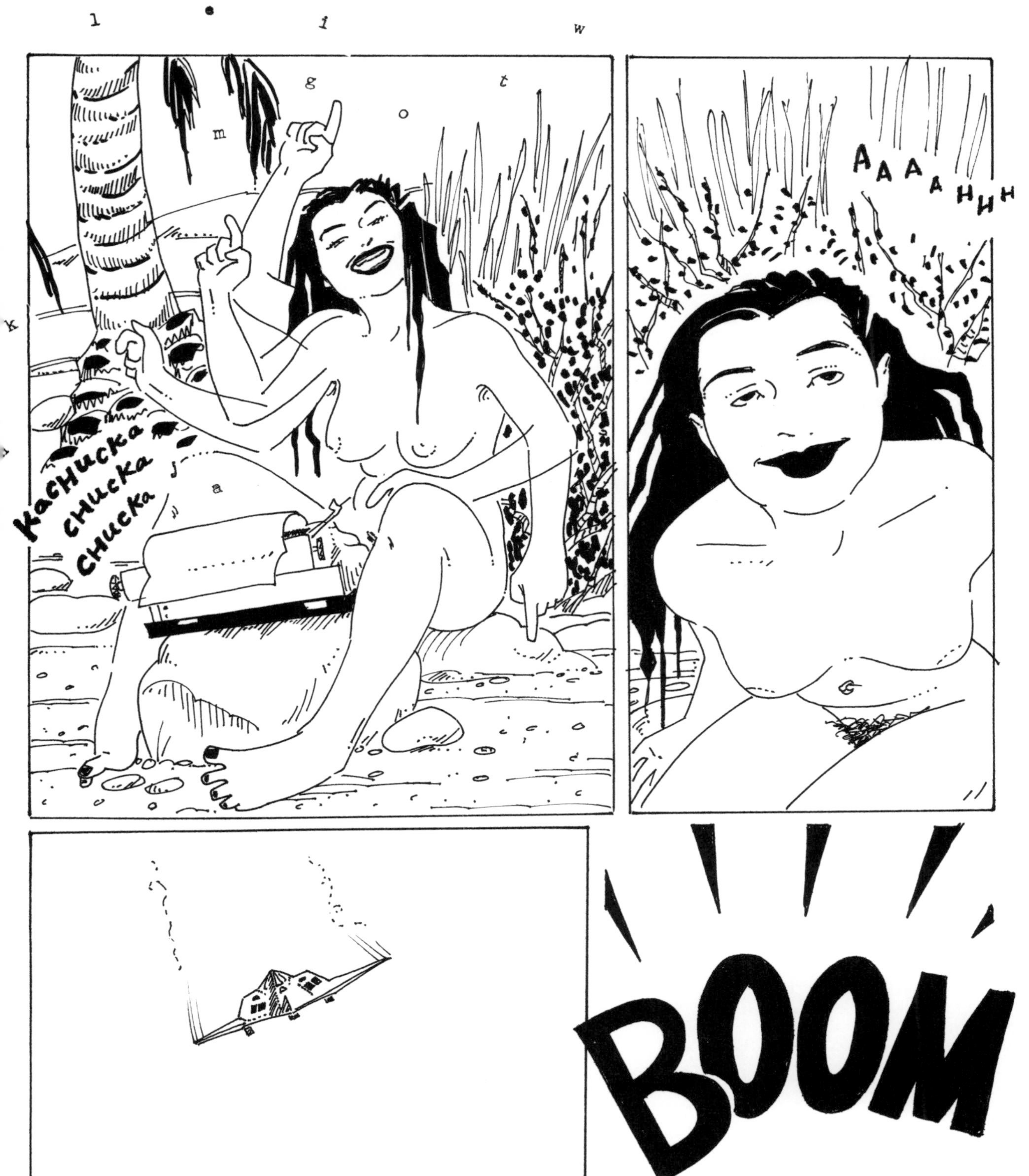
KACHUCKA
CHUCKA
CHUCKA
AAAAHHH
BOOM

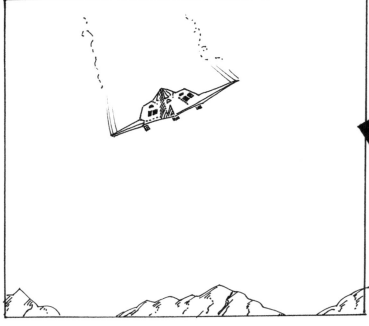

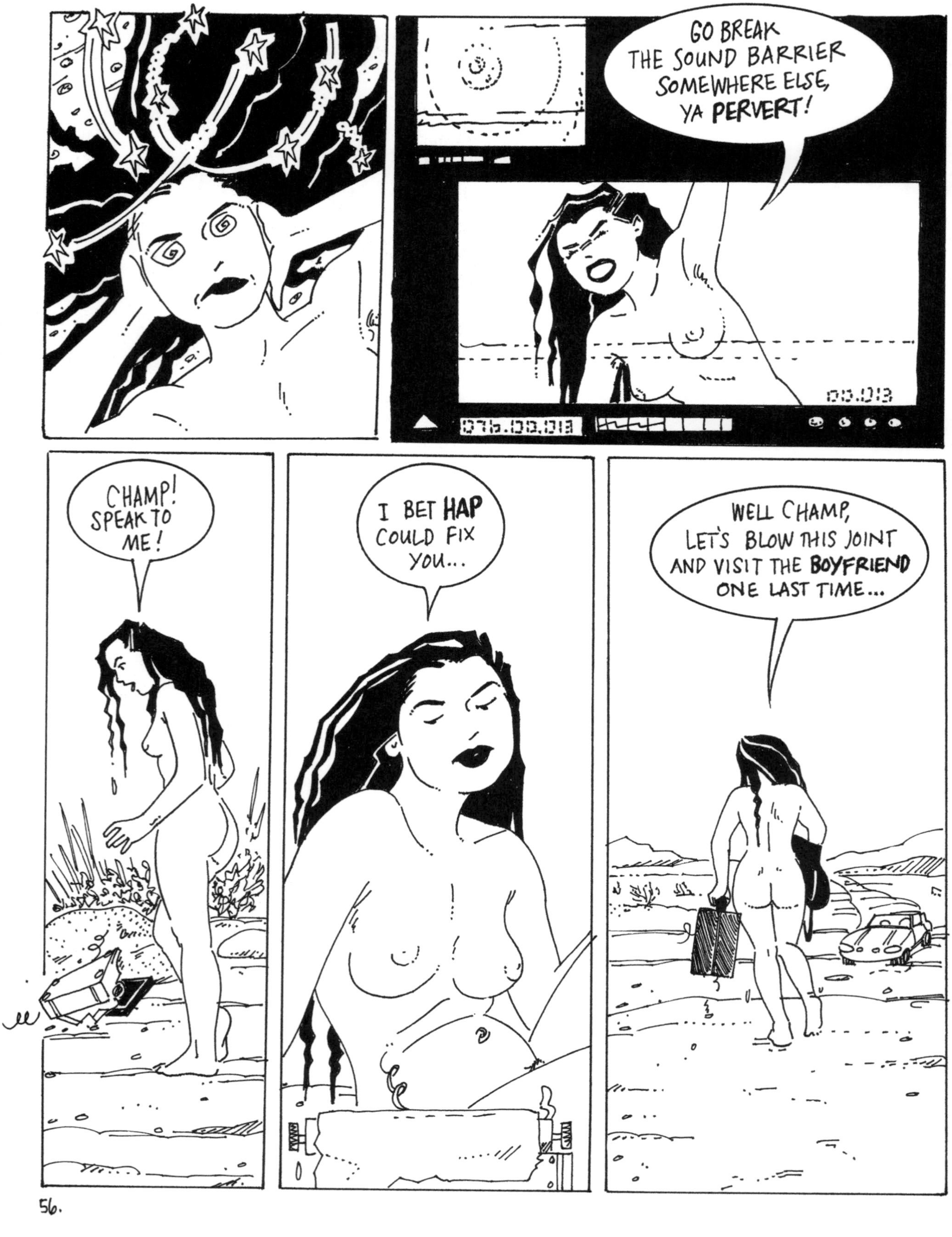
GO BREAK THE SOUND BARRIER SOMEWHERE ELSE, YA **PERVERT**!
00.013
076.00.013
CHAMP! SPEAK TO ME!
I BET **HAP** COULD FIX YOU...
WELL CHAMP, LET'S BLOW THIS JOINT AND VISIT THE **BOYFRIEND** ONE LAST TIME...

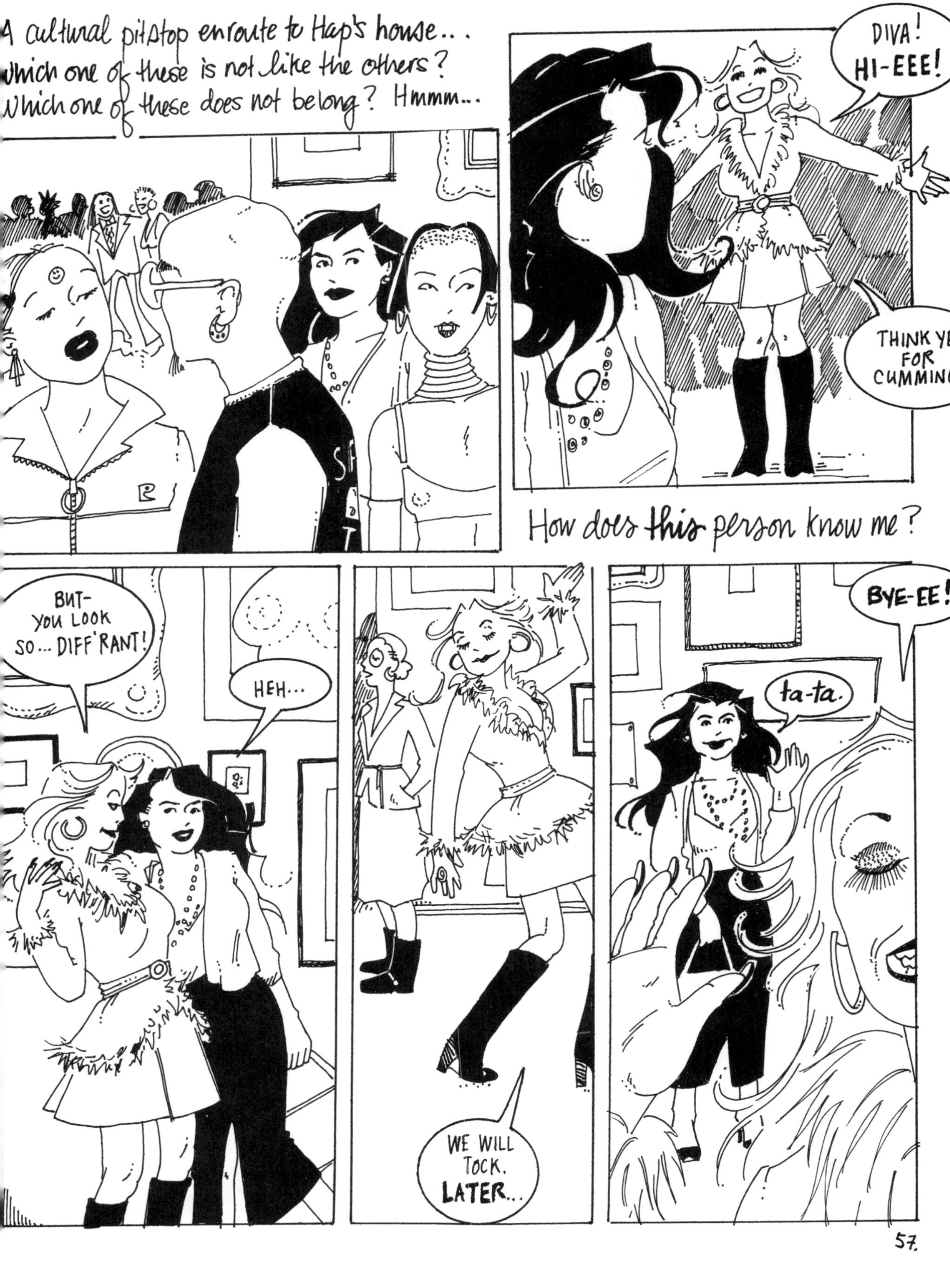

A cultural pitstop enroute to Hap's house...
Which one of these is not like the others?
Which one of these does not belong? Hmmm...
DIVA! HI-EEE!
THINK YEW FOR CUMMING!
How does this person know me?
BUT- YOU LOOK SO... DIFF'RANT!
HEH...
WE WILL TOCK. LATER...
BYE-EE!
ta-ta.

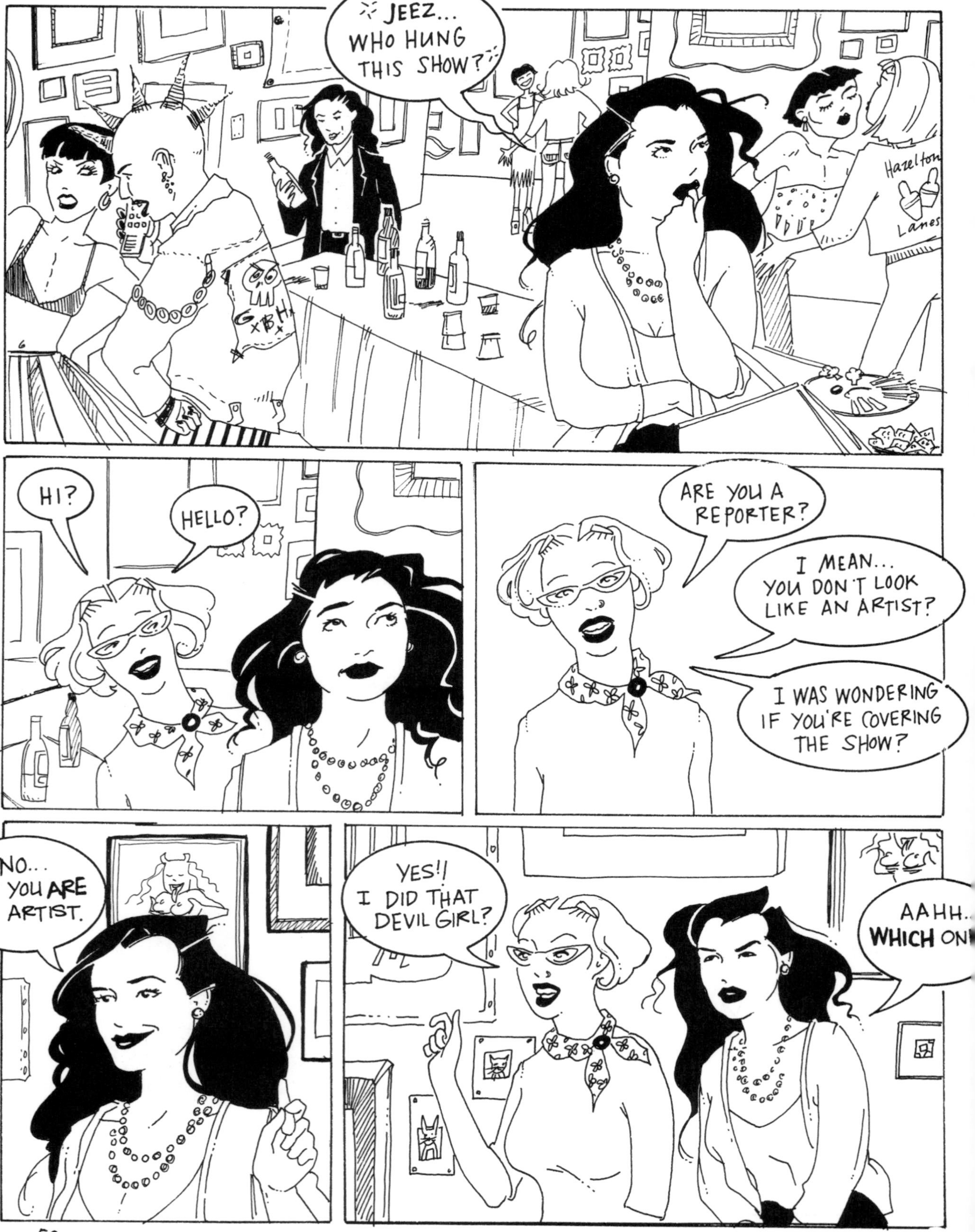
JEEZ... WHO HUNG THIS SHOW?
Hazelton Lanes
HI?
HELLO?
ARE YOU A REPORTER?
I MEAN... YOU DON'T LOOK LIKE AN ARTIST?
I WAS WONDERING IF YOU'RE COVERING THE SHOW?
NO... BUT YOU **ARE** AN ARTIST.
YES!! I DID THAT DEVIL GIRL?
AAHH.. **WHICH** ON

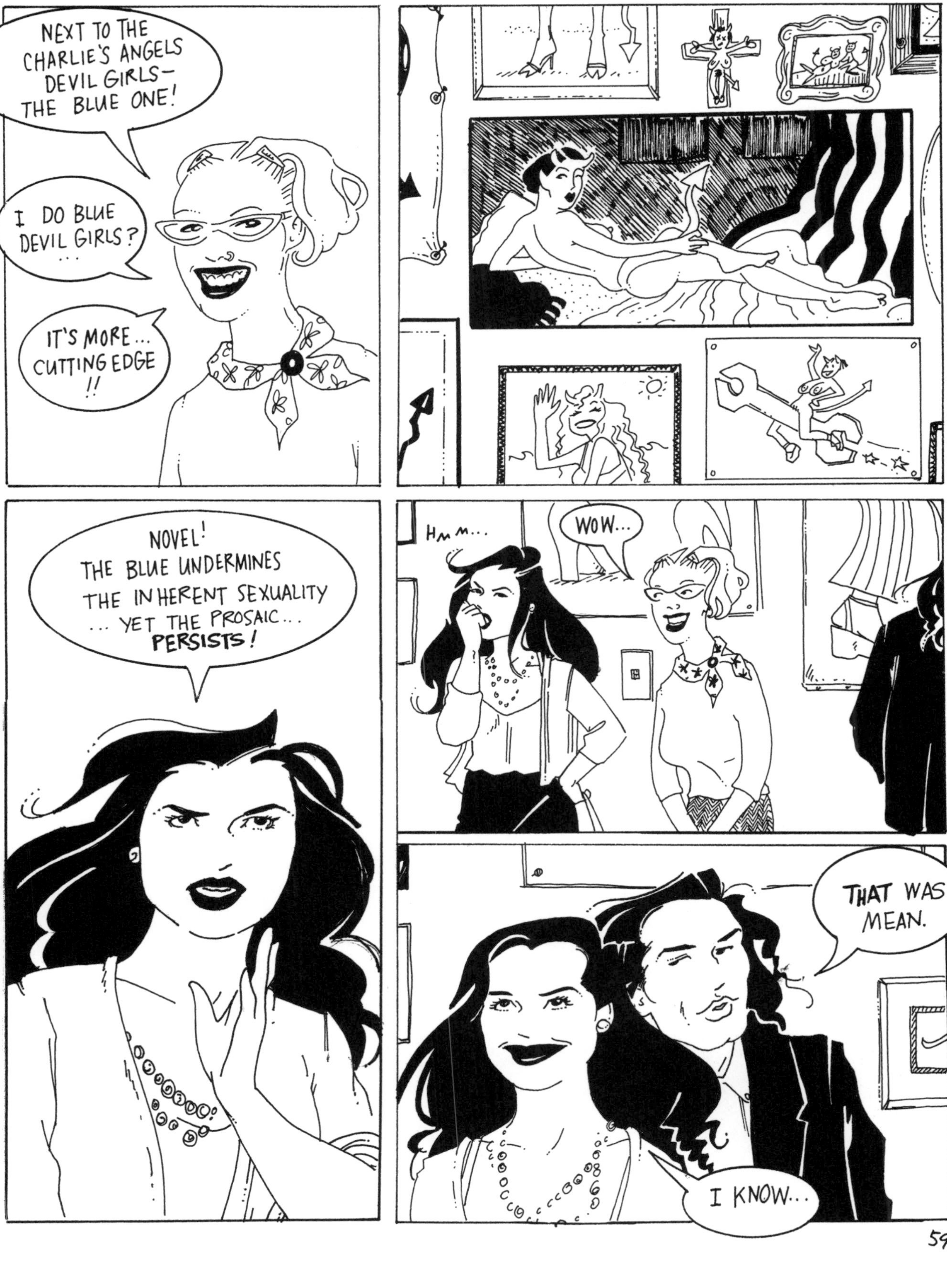
NEXT TO THE CHARLIE'S ANGELS DEVIL GIRLS— THE BLUE ONE!
I DO BLUE DEVIL GIRLS? ...
IT'S MORE... CUTTING EDGE !!
NOVEL! THE BLUE UNDERMINES THE INHERENT SEXUALITY ... YET THE PROSAIC... **PERSISTS**!
HMM...
WOW...
THAT WAS MEAN.
I KNOW...

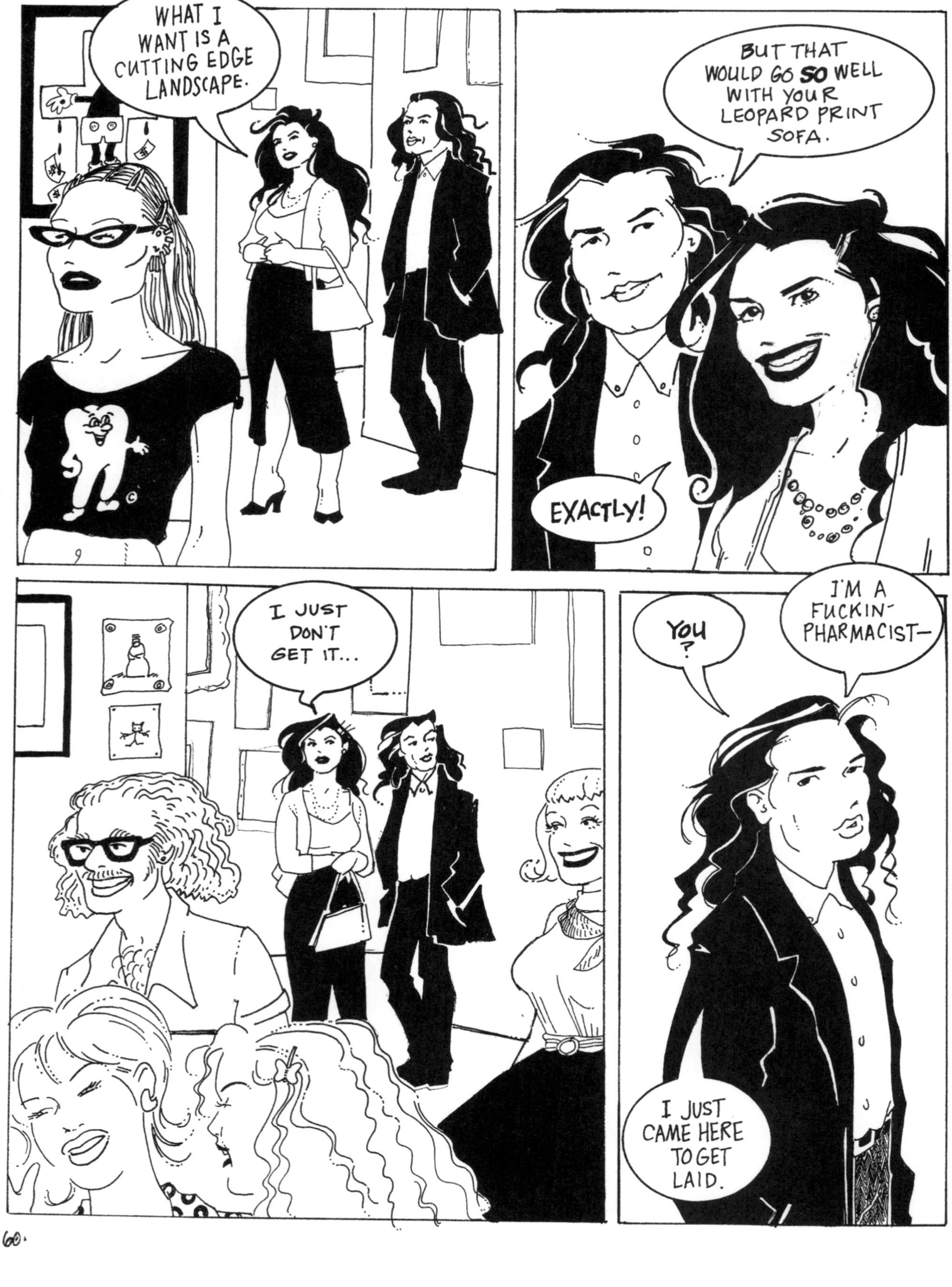
WHAT I WANT IS A CUTTING EDGE LANDSCAPE.
BUT THAT WOULD GO **SO** WELL WITH YOUR LEOPARD PRINT SOFA.
EXACTLY!
I JUST DON'T GET IT...
YOU?
I'M A FUCKIN-PHARMACIST—
I JUST CAME HERE TO GET LAID.

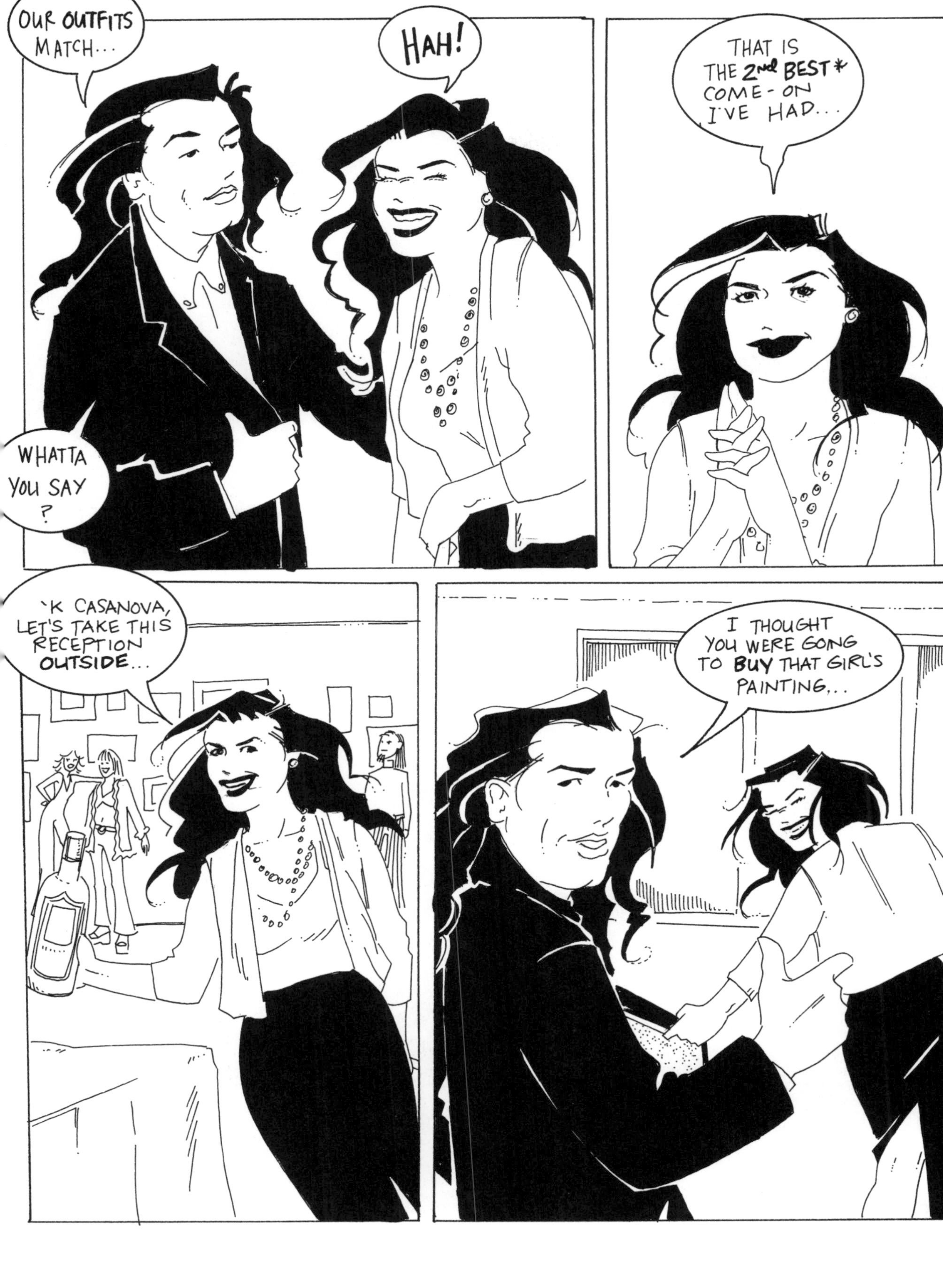
OUR OUTFITS MATCH...
HAH!
WHATTA YOU SAY ?
THAT IS THE 2nd BEST* COME-ON I'VE HAD...
`K CASANOVA, LET'S TAKE THIS RECEPTION OUTSIDE...
I THOUGHT YOU WERE GOING TO BUY THAT GIRL'S PAINTING,..

*See page 33 for number one

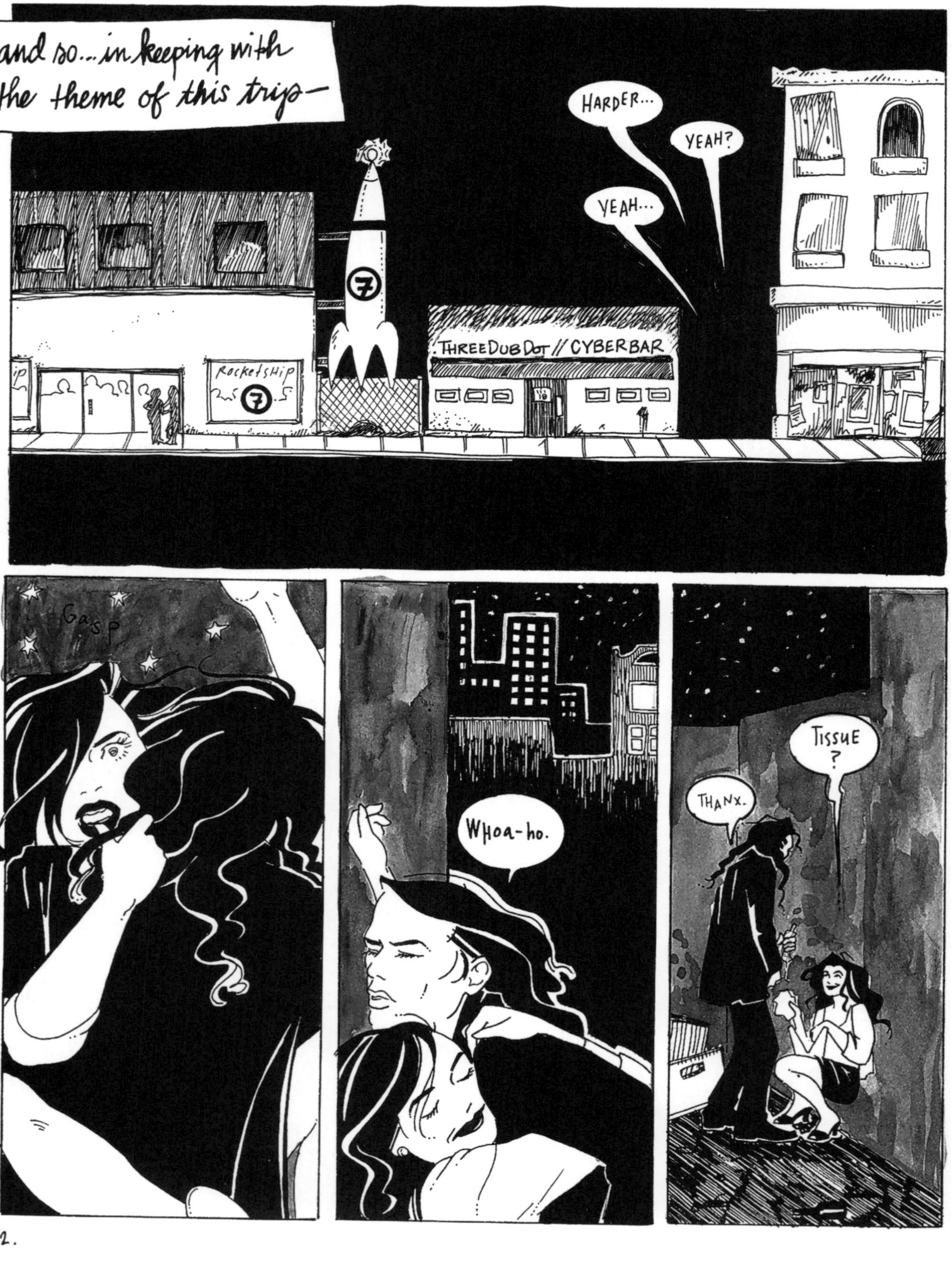
and so... in keeping with the theme of this trip—
HARDER...
YEAH?
YEAH...
ROCKETSHIP
THREEDUBDOT // CYBERBAR
GASP
WHOA-HO.
TISSUE?
THANX.

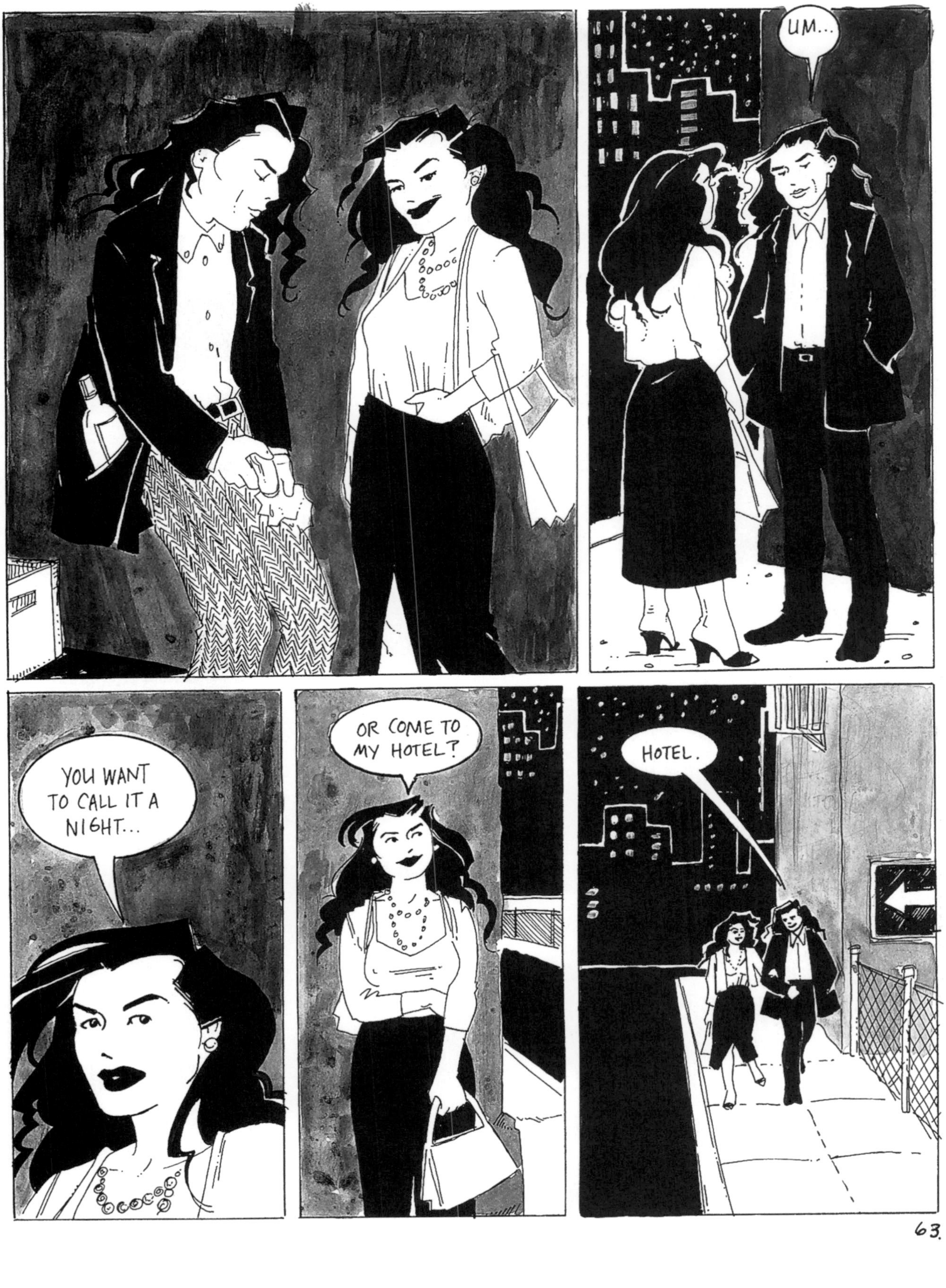
UM...
YOU WANT TO CALL IT A NIGHT...
OR COME TO MY HOTEL?
HOTEL.

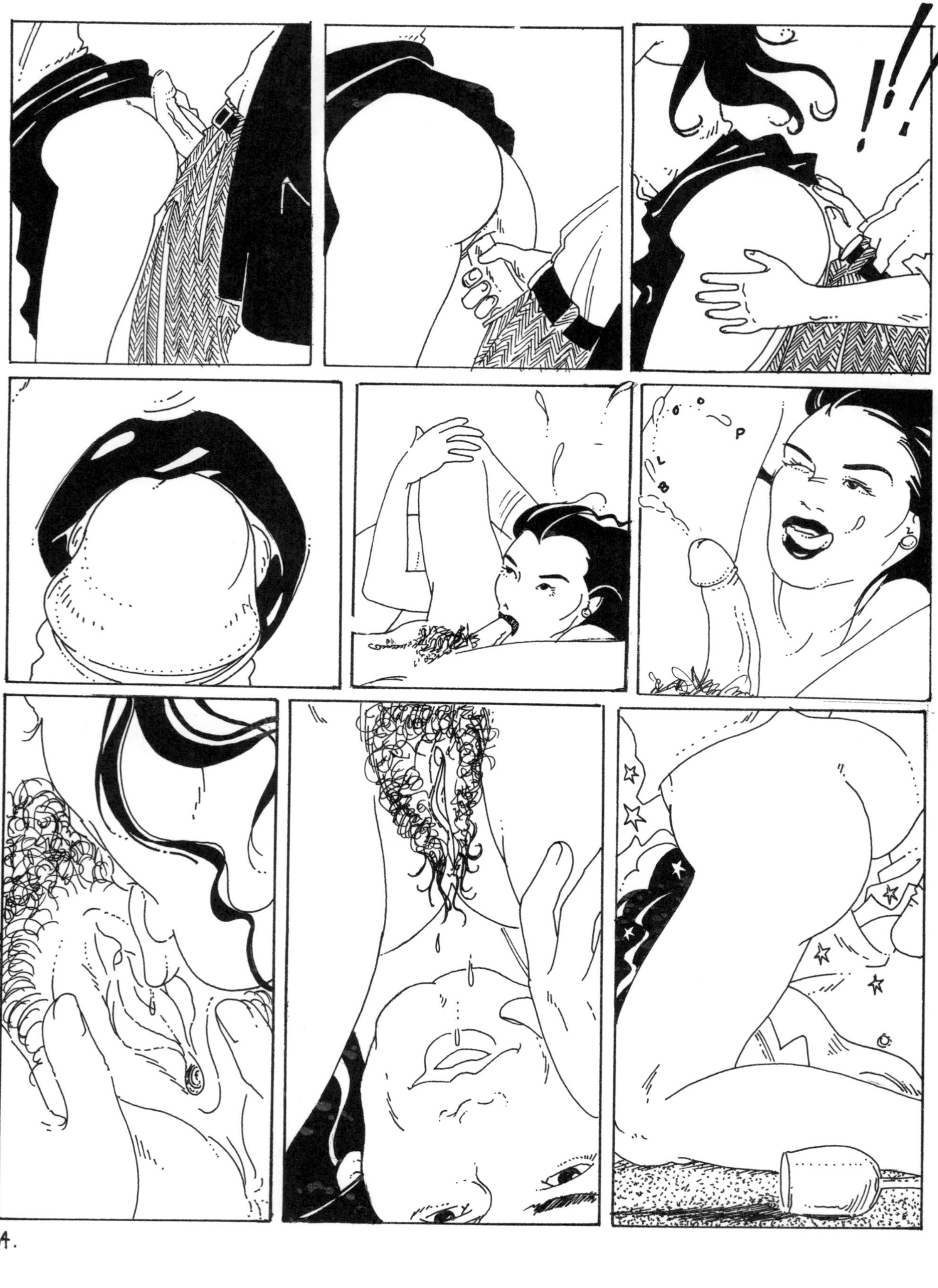
!!!
BLOOP

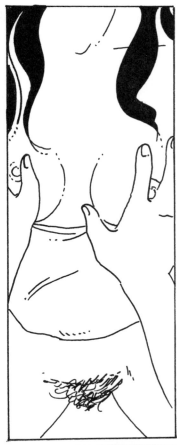

COME TO BED, SLEEPYHEAD.

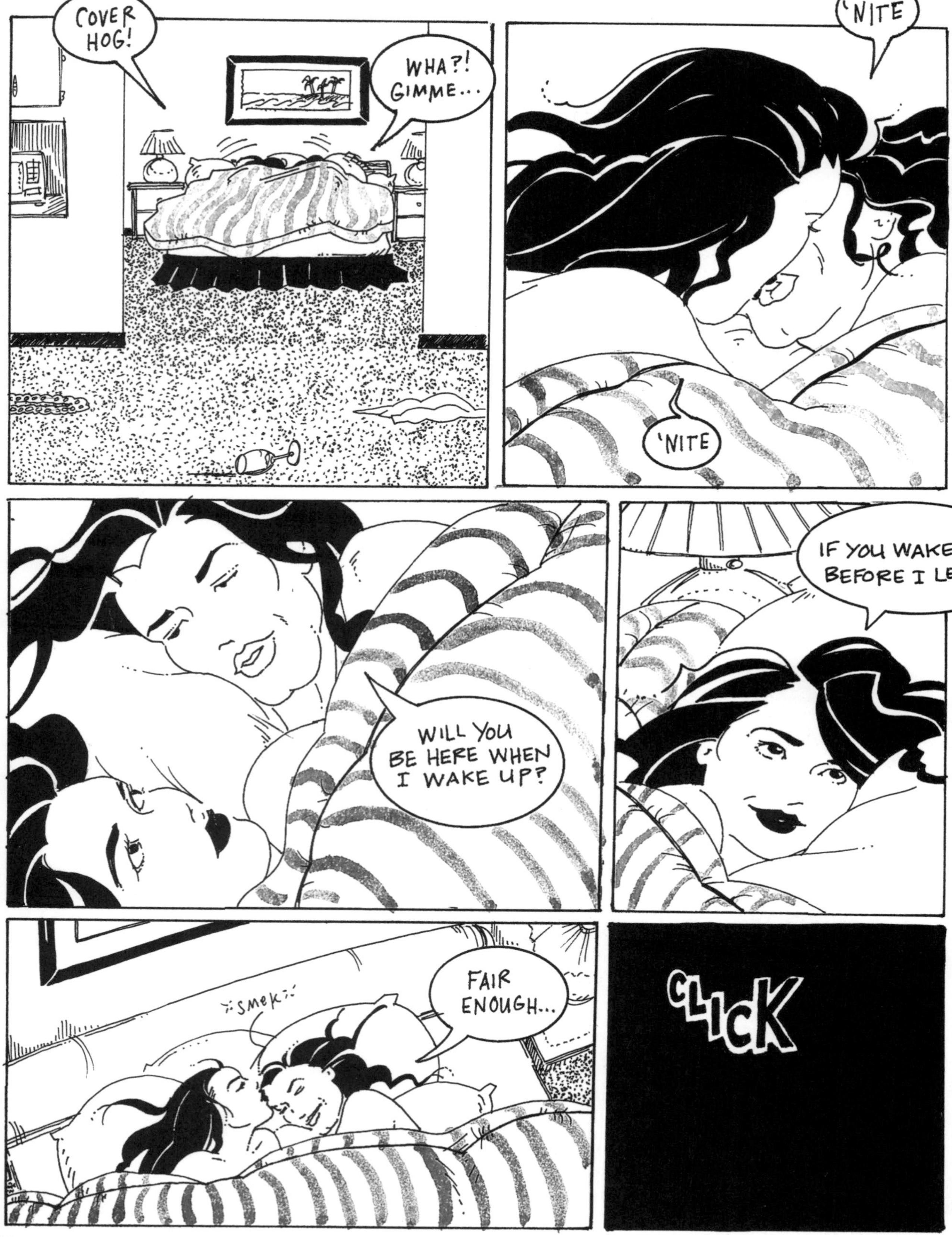
COVER HOG!
WHA?! GIMME...
'NITE
'NITE
WILL YOU BE HERE WHEN I WAKE UP?
IF YOU WAKE UP BEFORE I LEAVE.
:SMEK:
FAIR ENOUGH...
CLICK

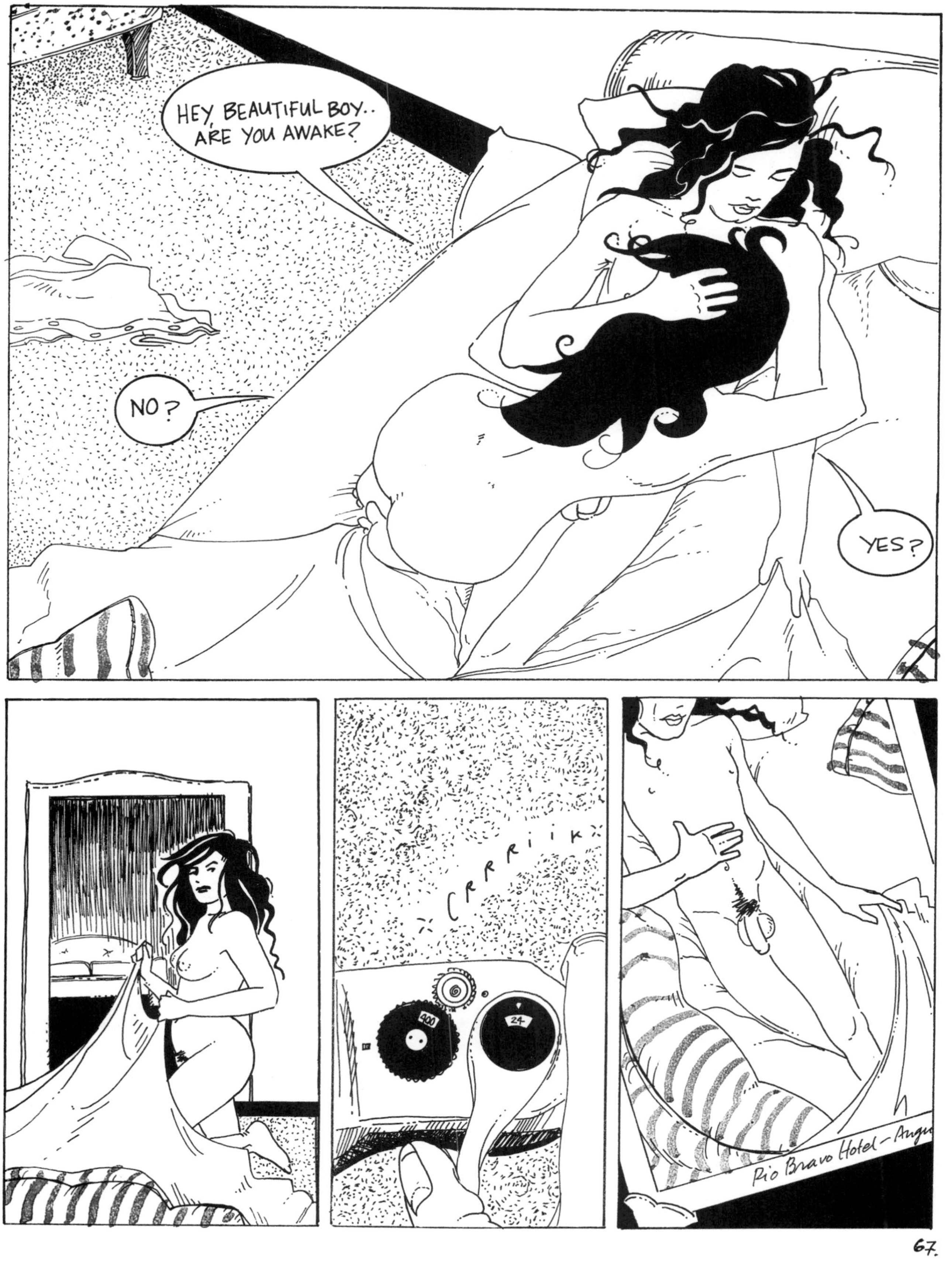
HEY, BEAUTIFUL BOY.. ARE YOU AWAKE?
NO?
YES?
CRRRIIK
400
24
Rio Bravo Hotel - Augu

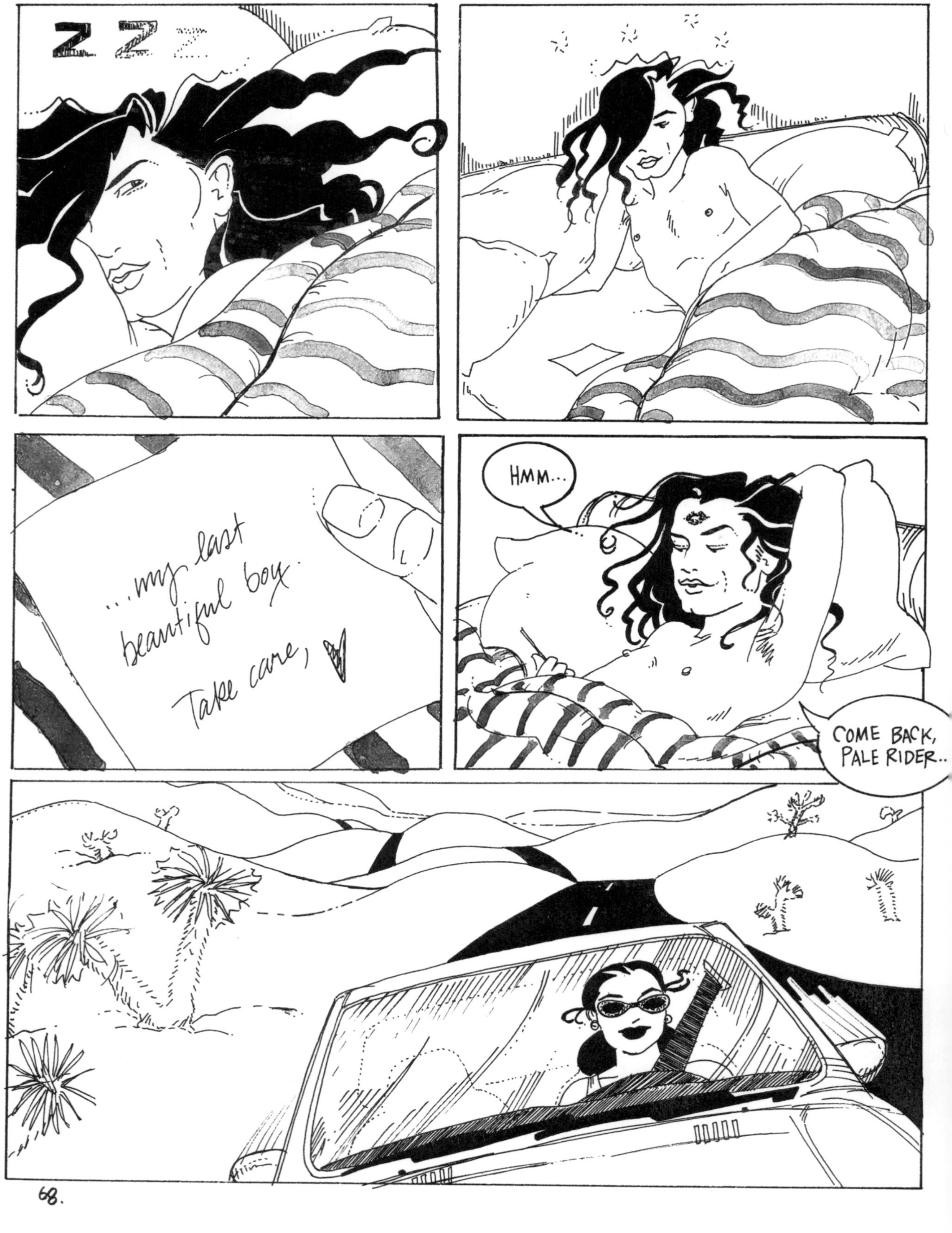
Z Z Z
...my last beautiful boy.
Take care,
HMM...
COME BACK, PALE RIDER...

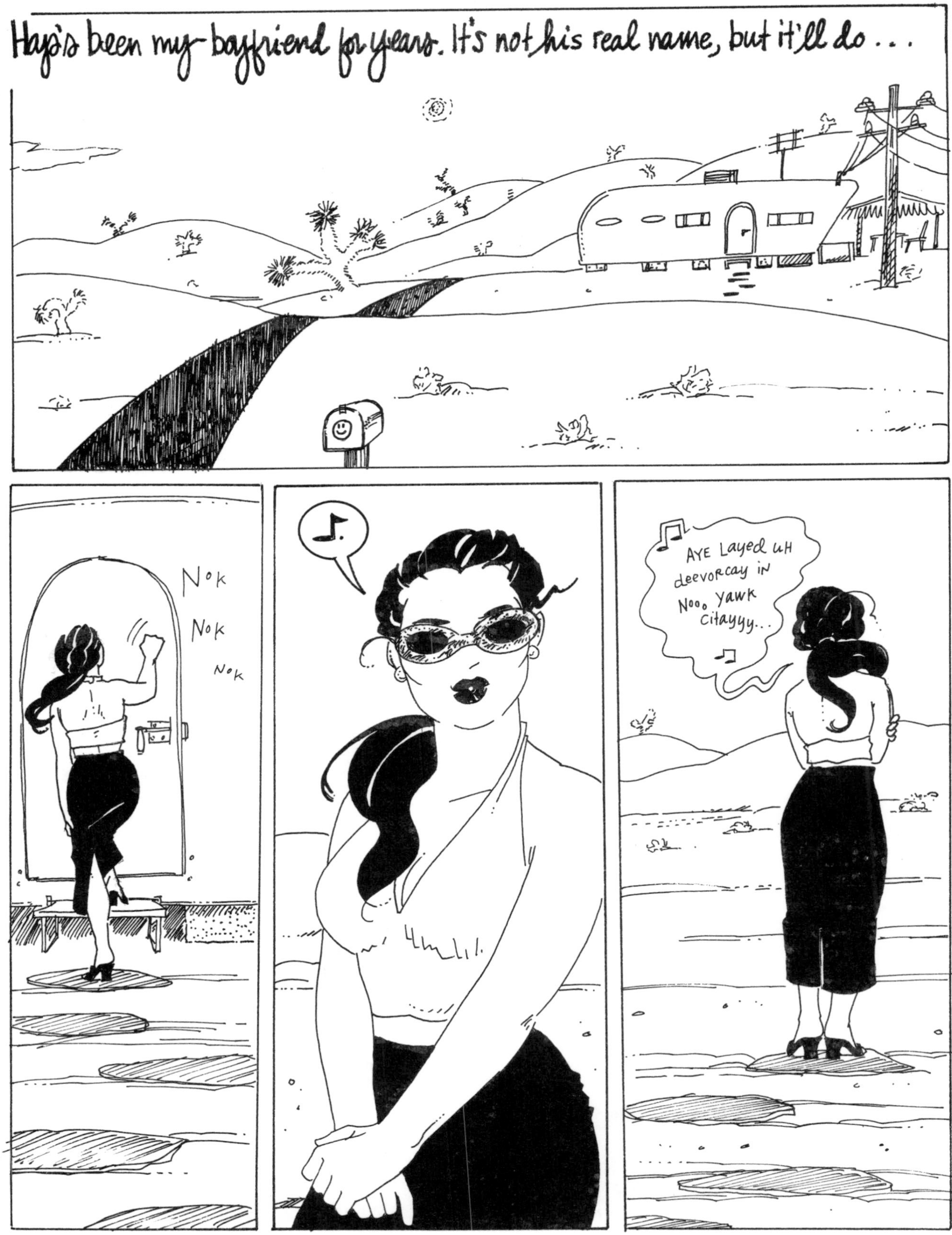

Hap's been my boyfriend for years. It's not his real name, but it'll do . . .
NOK
NOK
NOK
AYE Layed uH deevorcay iN Nooo yawk citayyy...

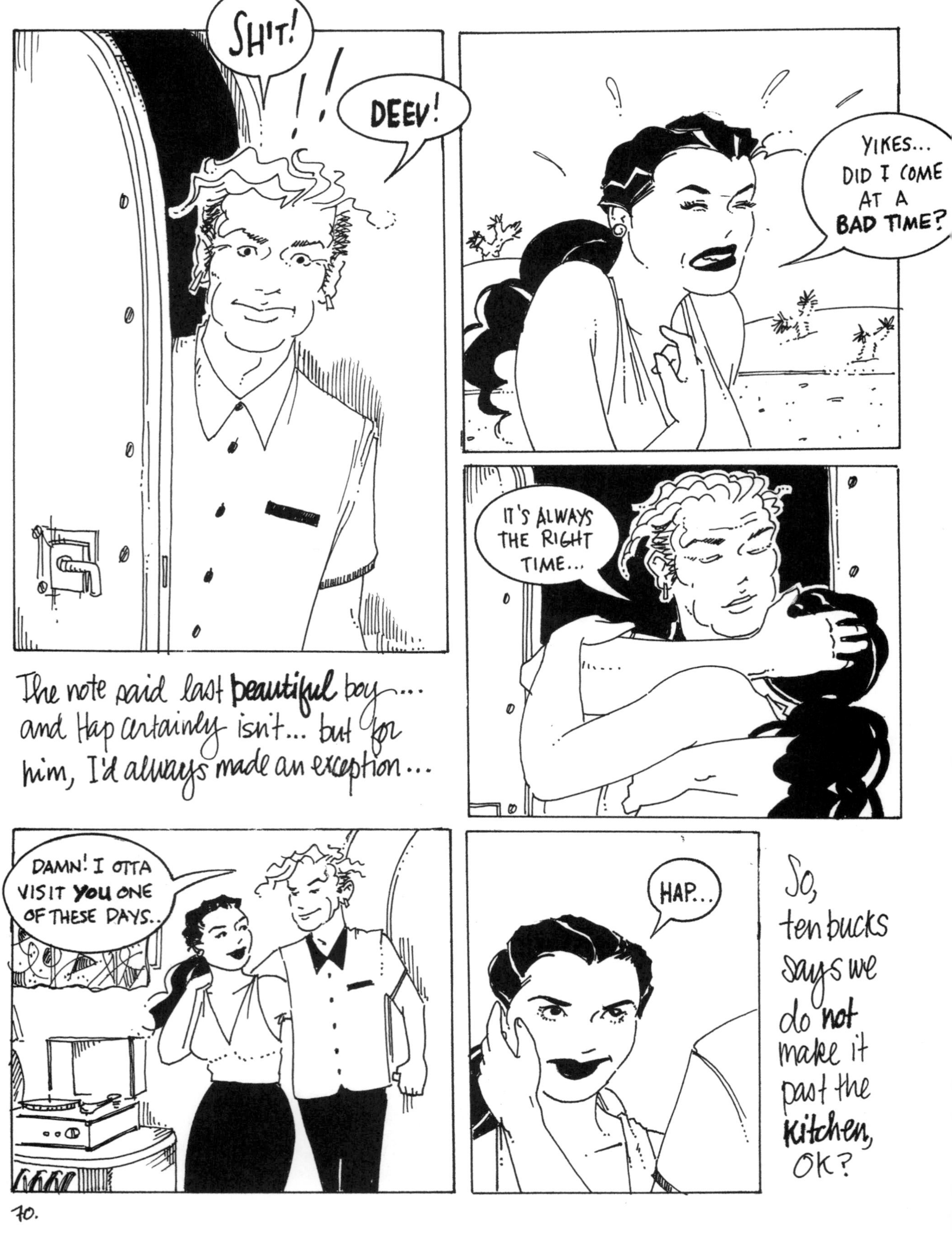
SHIT!
DEEV!
YIKES... DID I COME AT A BAD TIME?
IT'S ALWAYS THE RIGHT TIME...
The note said last beautiful boy... and Hap certainly isn't... but for him, I'd always made an exception...
DAMN! I OTTA VISIT YOU ONE OF THESE DAYS..
HAP...
So, ten bucks says we do not make it past the Kitchen, OK?

tink
tink

Hap swears that he can't even make himself
a cup of tea without getting a stiffy...

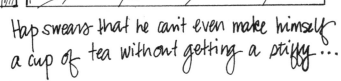

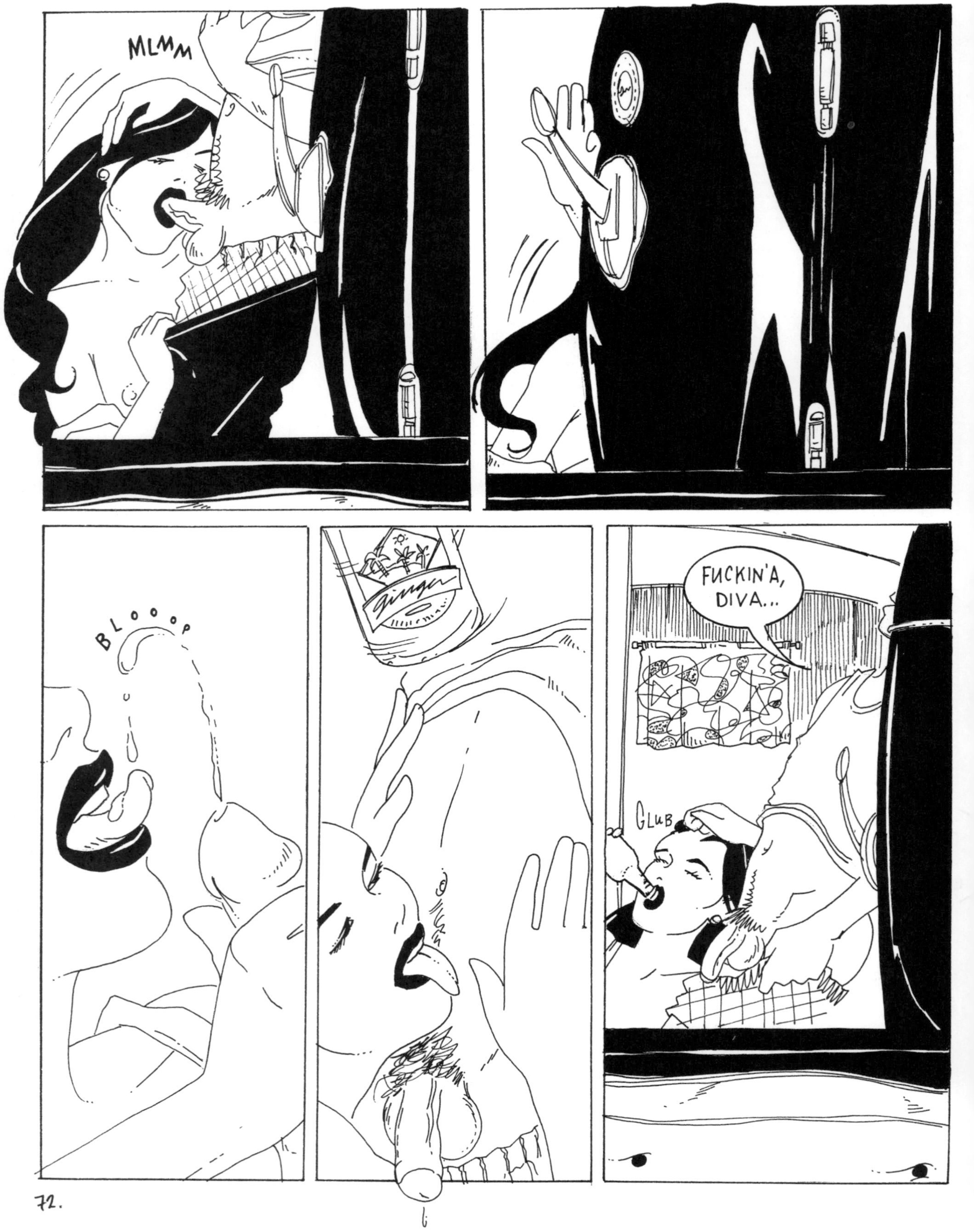
MLMM
BLOOOP
FUCKIN'A, DIVA...
GLUB

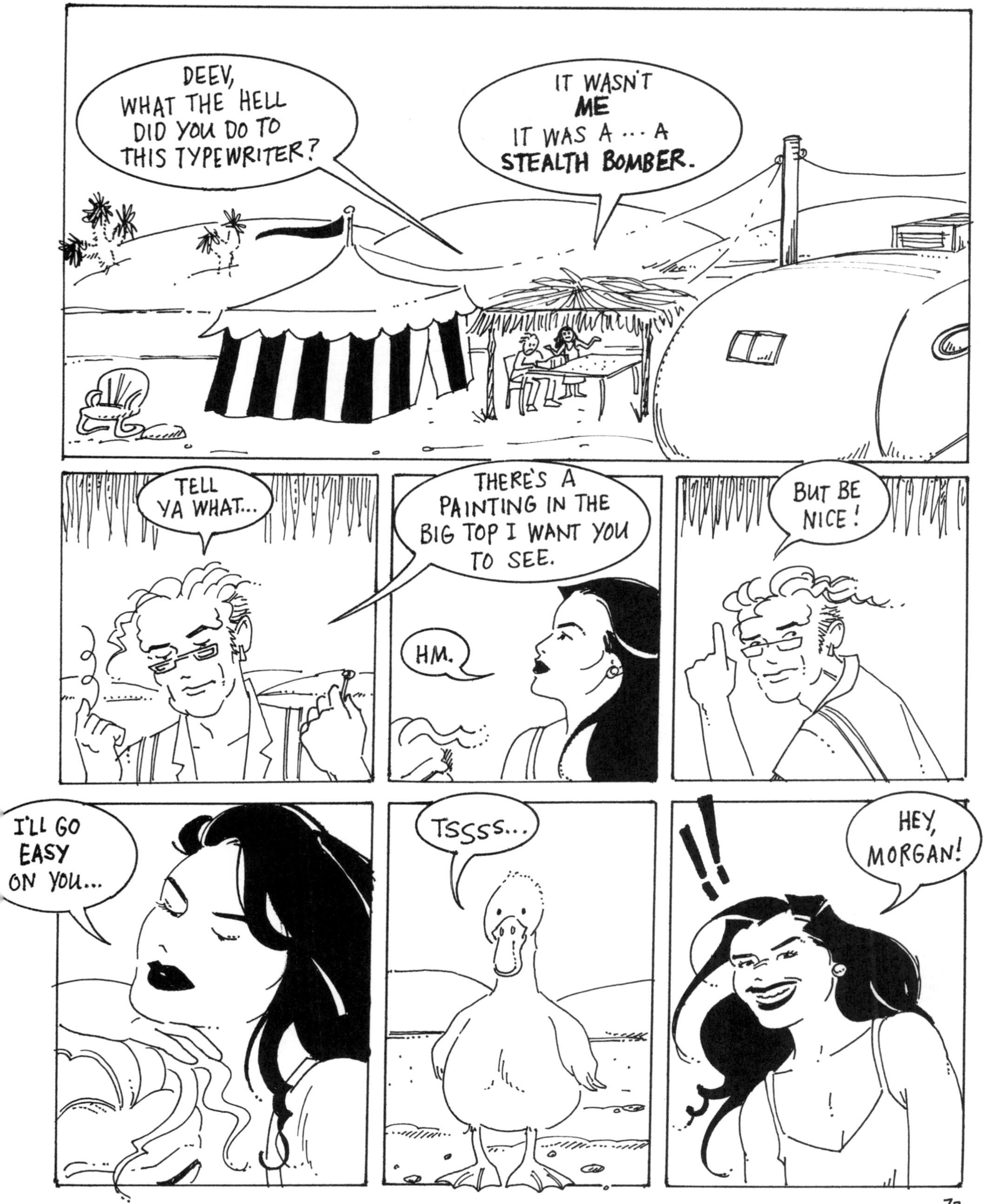
DEEV, WHAT THE HELL DID YOU DO TO THIS TYPEWRITER?
IT WASN'T ME IT WAS A ... A STEALTH BOMBER.
TELL YA WHAT...
THERE'S A PAINTING IN THE BIG TOP I WANT YOU TO SEE.
HM.
BUT BE NICE!
I'LL GO EASY ON YOU...
TSSSS...
!!
HEY, MORGAN!

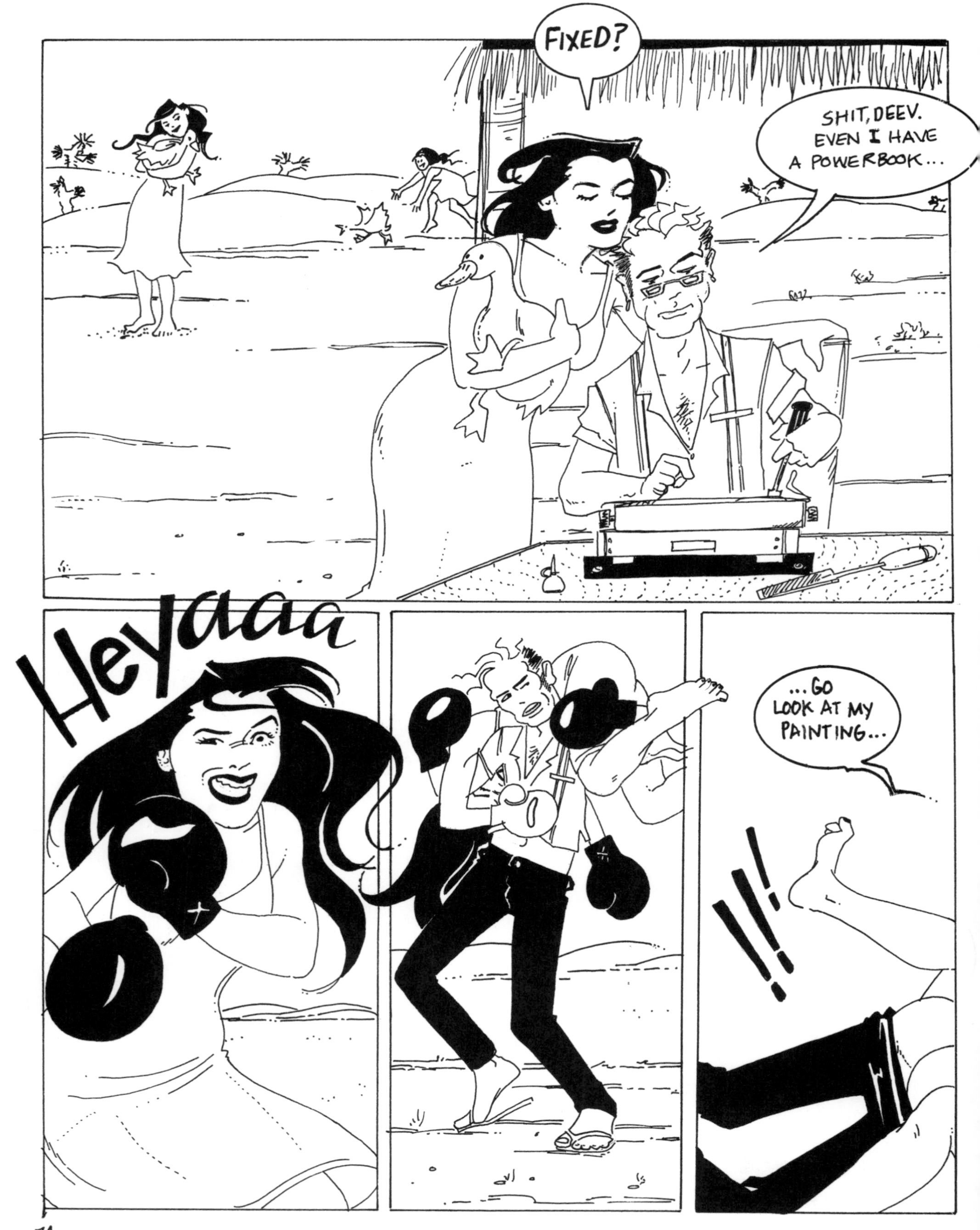
FIXED?
SHIT, DEEV. EVEN I HAVE A POWERBOOK...
Heyaaa
...GO LOOK AT MY PAINTING...
!!!

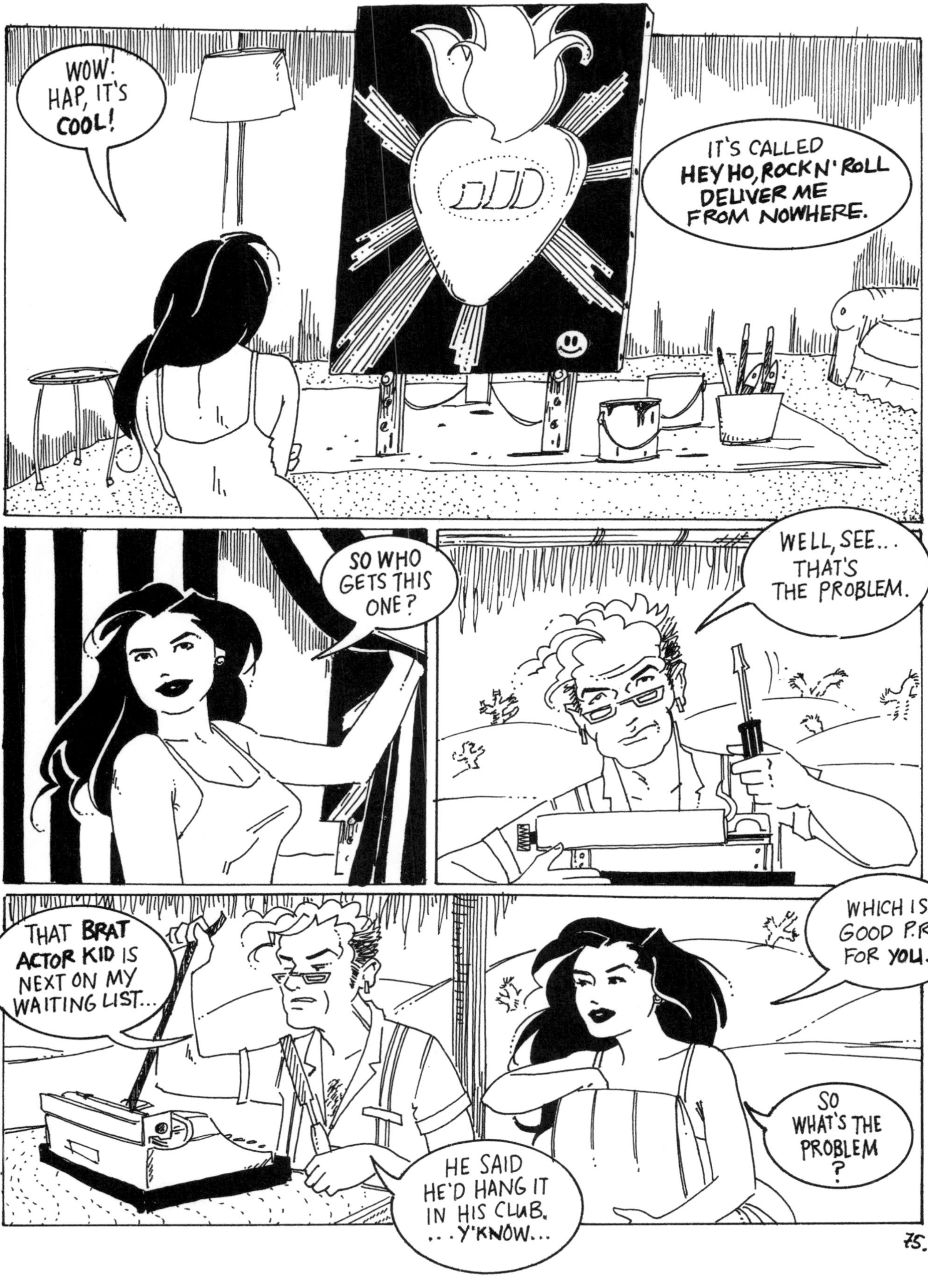
WOW! HAP, IT'S COOL!
IT'S CALLED HEY HO, ROCK N' ROLL DELIVER ME FROM NOWHERE.
SO WHO GETS THIS ONE?
WELL, SEE... THAT'S THE PROBLEM.
THAT BRAT ACTOR KID IS NEXT ON MY WAITING LIST...
WHICH IS GOOD P.R. FOR YOU...
SO WHAT'S THE PROBLEM?
HE SAID HE'D HANG IT IN HIS CLUB. ...Y'KNOW...

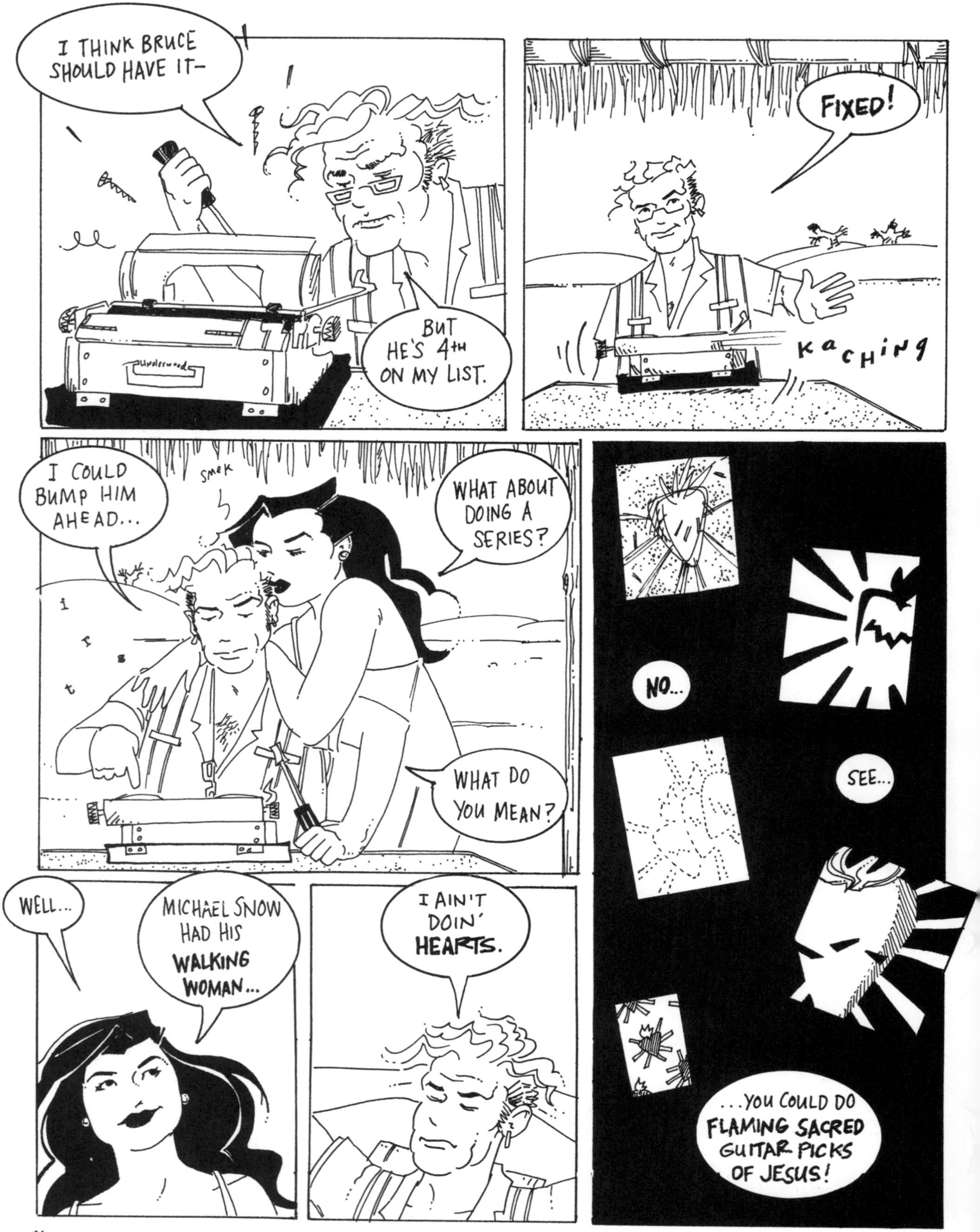
I THINK BRUCE SHOULD HAVE IT-
BUT HE'S 4TH ON MY LIST.
FIXED!
KACHING
I COULD BUMP HIM AHEAD...
smek
WHAT ABOUT DOING A SERIES?
WHAT DO YOU MEAN?
NO...
SEE...
WELL...
MICHAEL SNOW HAD HIS WALKING WOMAN...
I AIN'T DOIN' HEARTS.
...YOU COULD DO FLAMING SACRED GUITAR PICKS OF JESUS!

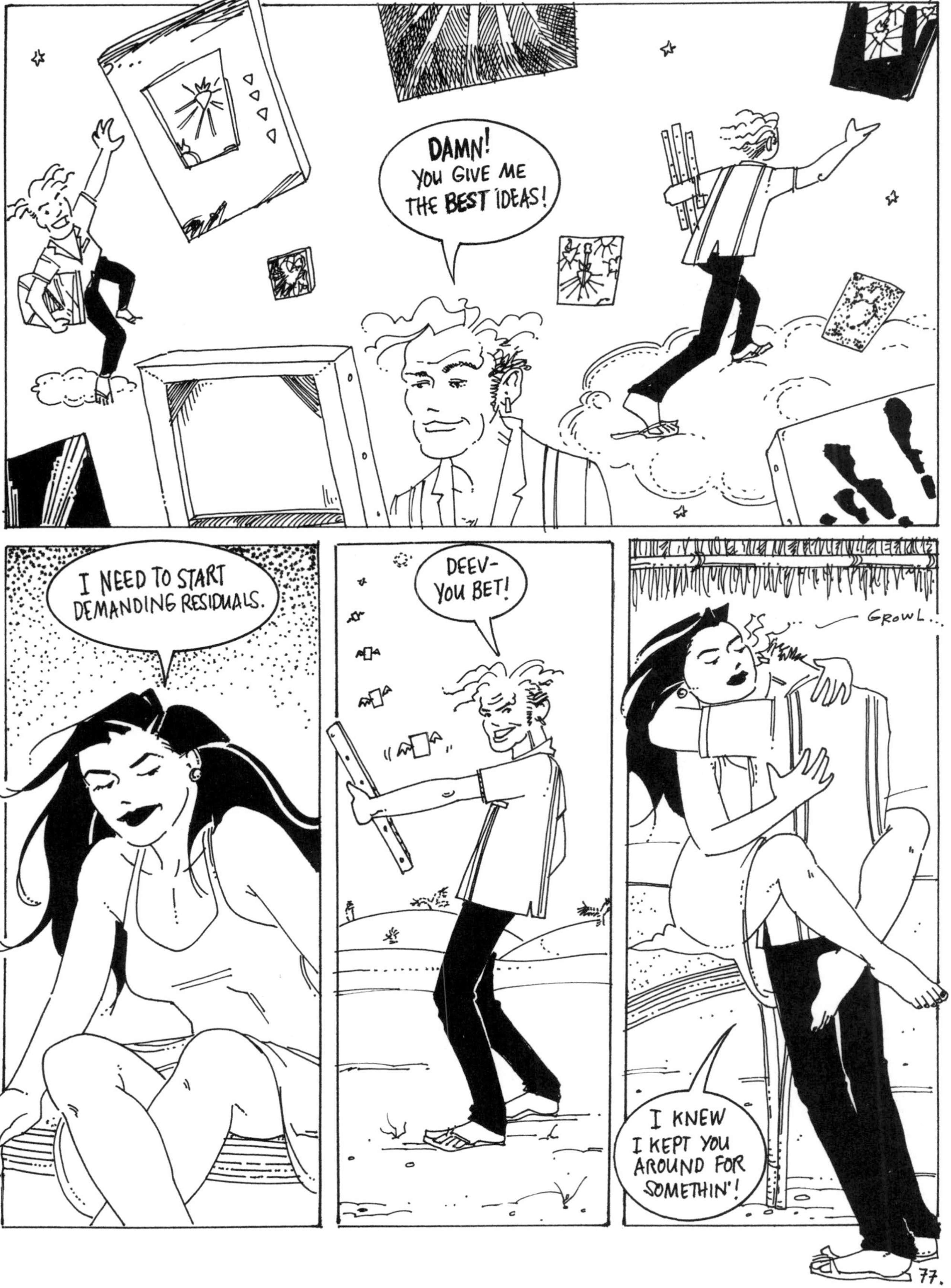
DAMN! YOU GIVE ME THE BEST IDEAS!
I NEED TO START DEMANDING RESIDUALS.
DEEV- YOU BET!
GROWL...
I KNEW I KEPT YOU AROUND FOR SOMETHIN'!

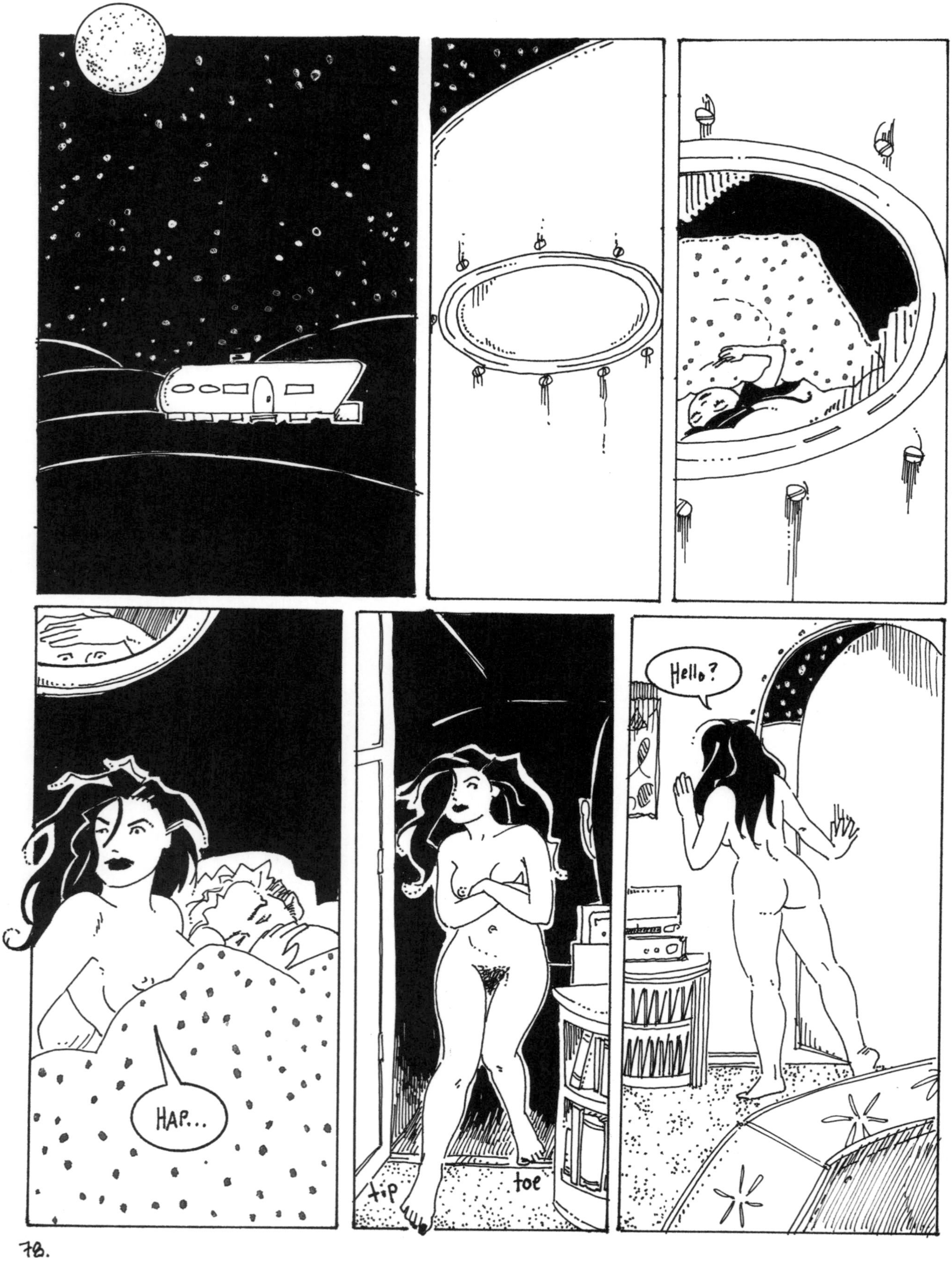
HAP...
tip
toe
Hello?

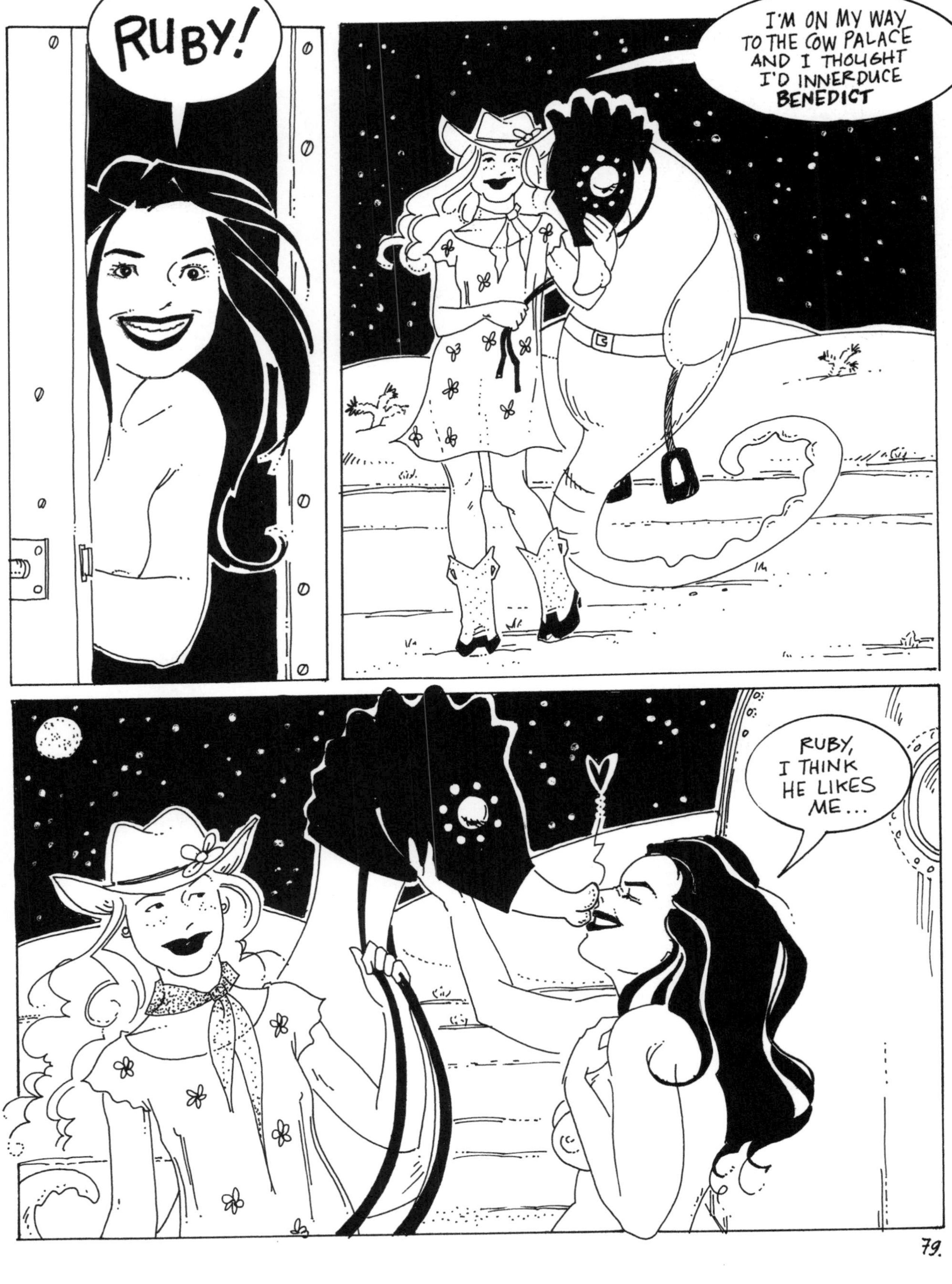
RUBY!
I'M ON MY WAY TO THE COW PALACE AND I THOUGHT I'D INNERDUCE **BENEDICT**
RUBY, I THINK HE LIKES ME...

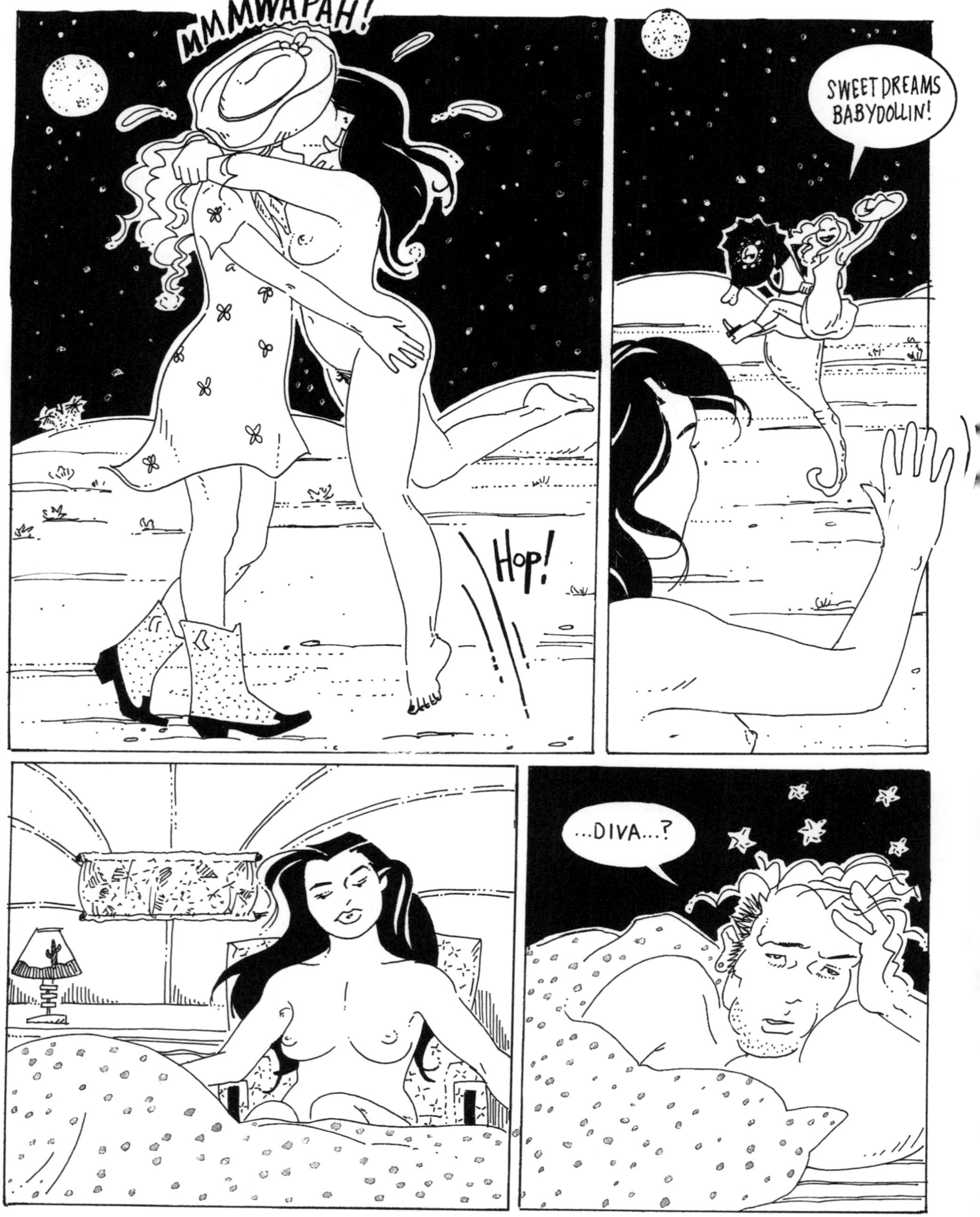
MMMWAPAH!
HOP!
SWEET DREAMS BABYDOLLIN!
...DIVA...?

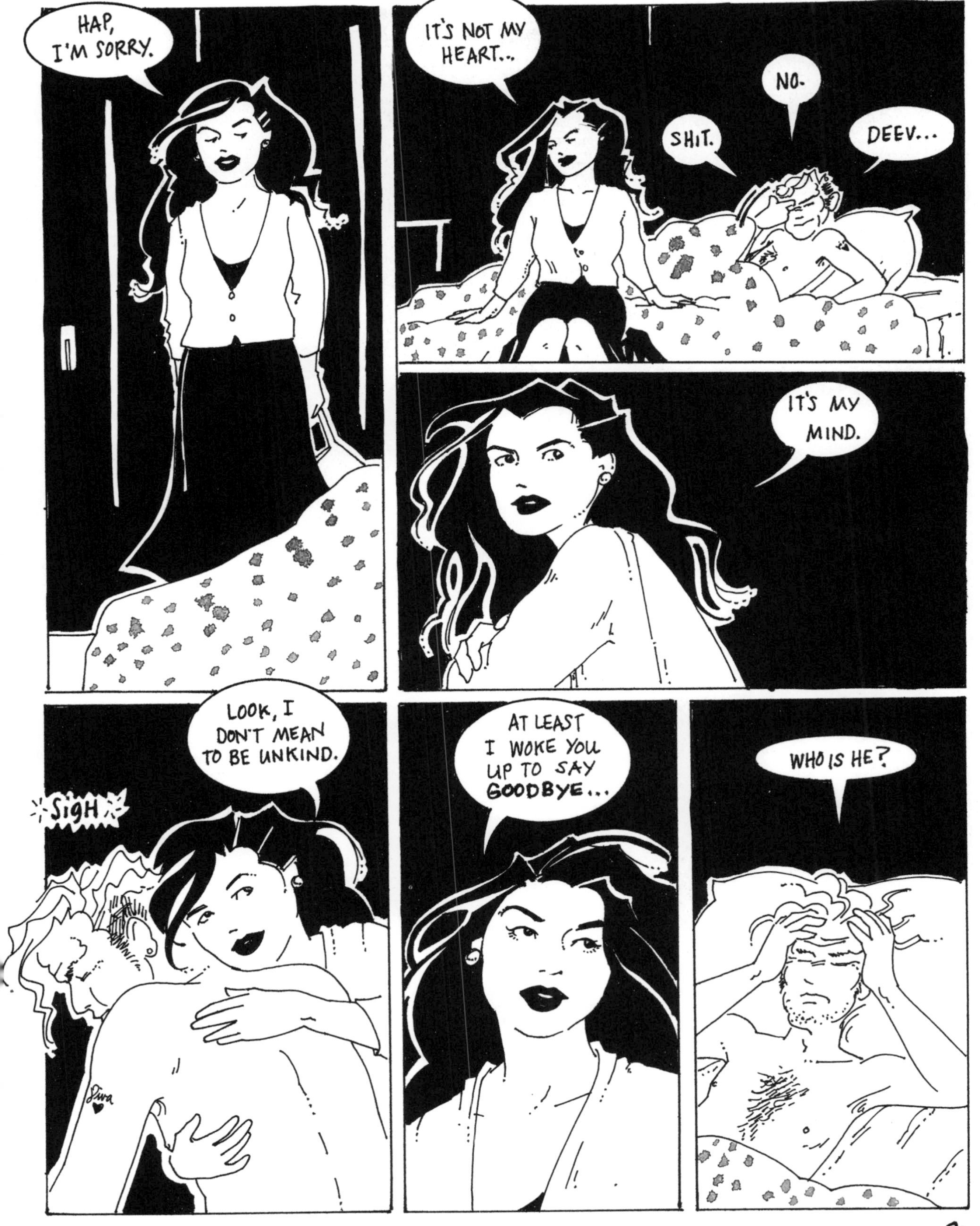
HAP, I'M SORRY.
IT'S NOT MY HEART...
SHIT.
NO.
DEEV...
IT'S MY MIND.
SIGH
LOOK, I DON'T MEAN TO BE UNKIND.
AT LEAST I WOKE YOU UP TO SAY GOODBYE...
WHO IS HE?

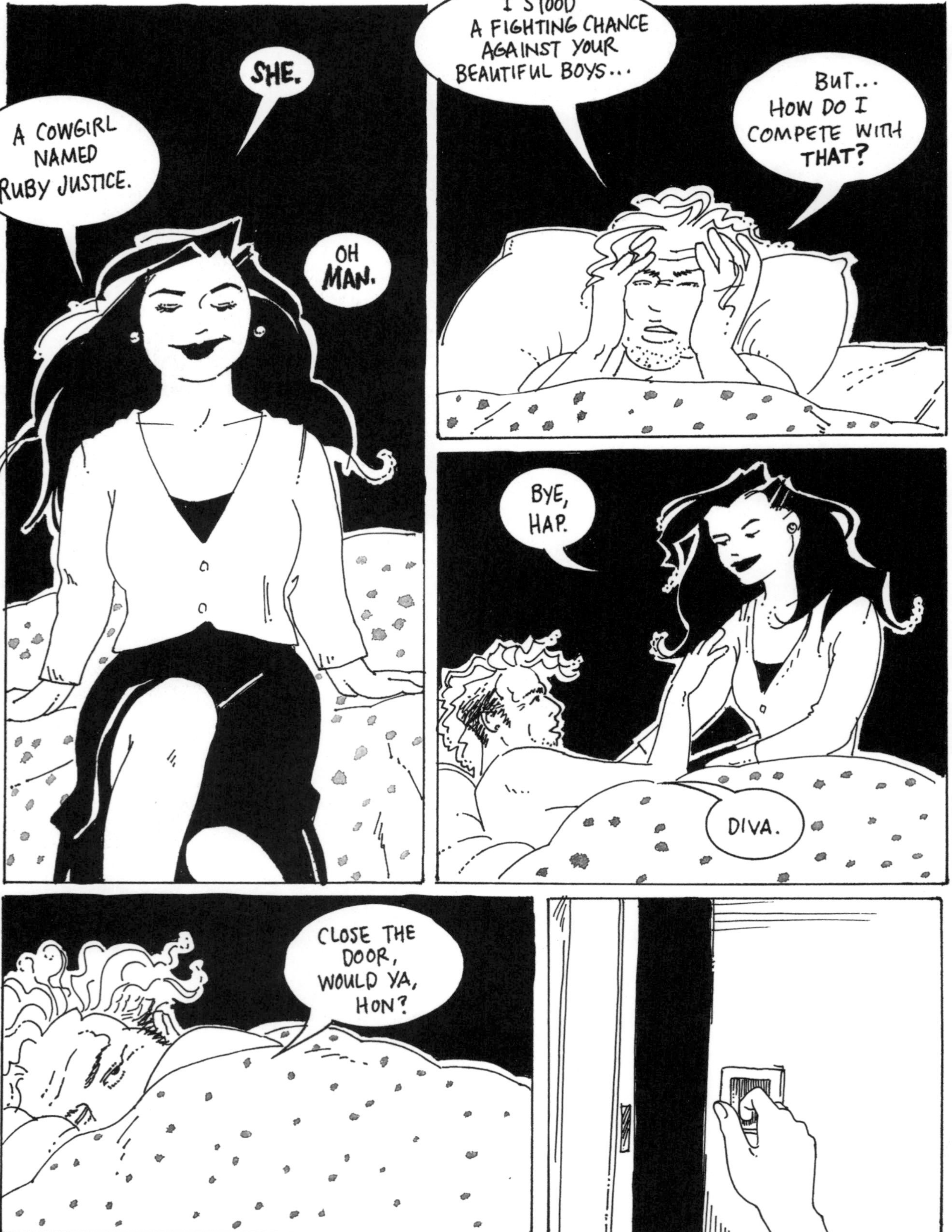
A COWGIRL NAMED RUBY JUSTICE.
SHE.
OH MAN.
I STOOD A FIGHTING CHANCE AGAINST YOUR BEAUTIFUL BOYS...
BUT... HOW DO I COMPETE WITH THAT?
BYE, HAP.
DIVA.
CLOSE THE DOOR, WOULD YA, HON?

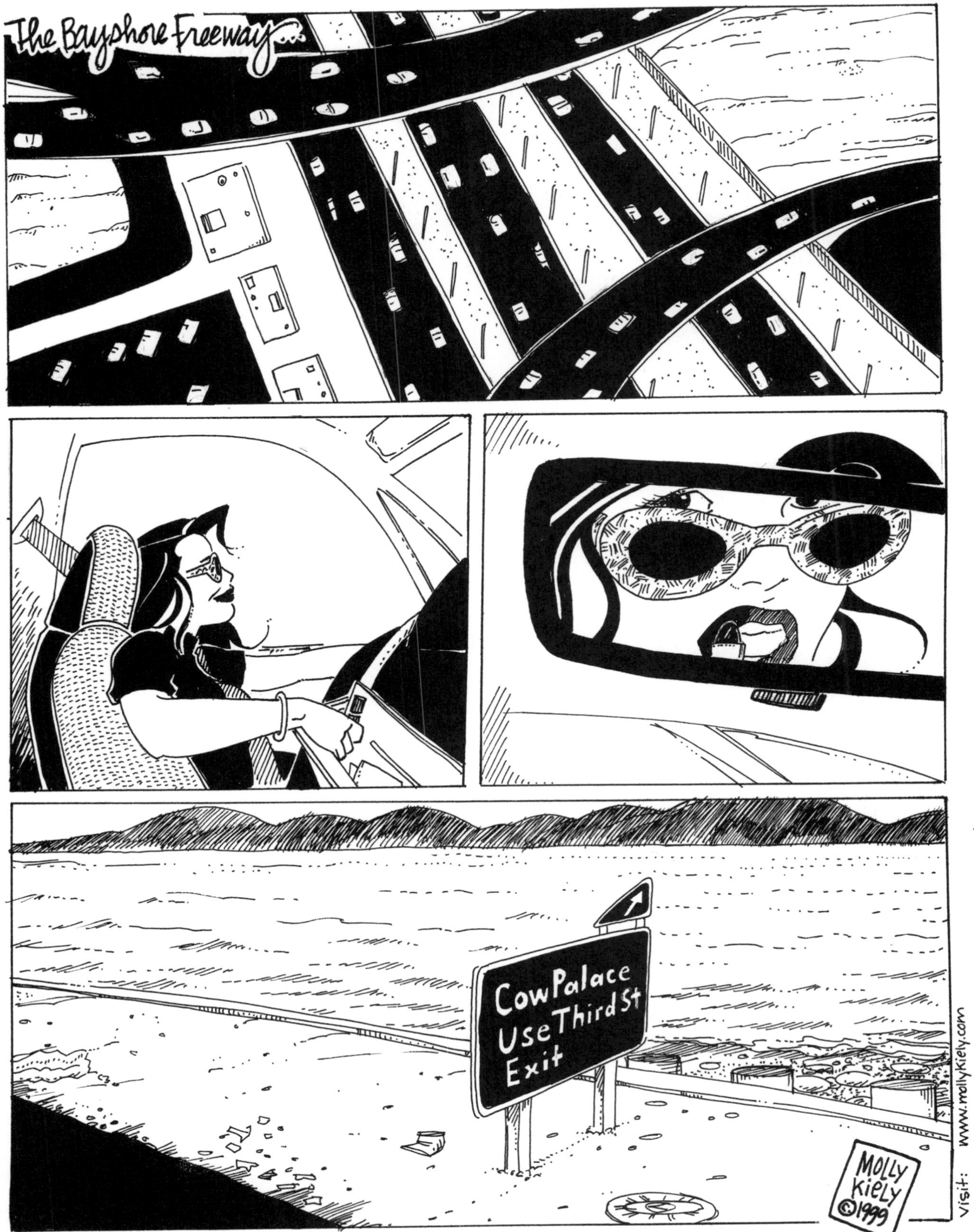
The Bayshore Freeway...
Cow Palace
Use Third St
Exit
MOLLY KIELY ©1999
visit: www.mollykiely.com